P9-CRG-783

WORKING WITH
DRYWALL

Creative Publishing
international

MINNEAPOLIS, MINNESOTA
www.creativepub.com

Creative Publishing international

Copyright © 2009
Creative Publishing international, Inc.
400 First Avenue North, Suite 300
Minneapolis, Minnesota 55401
1-800-328-0590
www.creativepub.com
All rights reserved

Printed in China

10 9 8 7 6 5 4

Library of Congress Cataloging-in-Publication Data

Working with drywall : hanging & finishing drywall the professional way.
   p. cm.
 Includes index.
 Summary: "A detailed and thorough guide to all the tools, materials
and techniques needed to hang and finish drywall with professional
results"--Provided by publisher.
  ISBN-13: 978-1-58923-477-2 (soft cover)
  ISBN-10: 1-58923-477-4 (soft cover)
  1. Drywall construction--Handbooks, manuals, etc. I. Creative
Publishing International. II. Title.

TH8139.W67 2009
693'.6--dc22

2009033592

President/CEO: Ken Fund

Home Improvement Group

Publisher: Bryan Trandem
Managing Editor: Tracy Stanley
Senior Editor: Mark Johanson
Editor: Jennifer Gehlhar

Creative Director: Michele Lanci-Altomare
Senior Design Managers: Jon Simpson, Brad Springer
Design Managers: James Kegley

Lead Photographer: Joel Schnell
Shop Manager: James Parmeter

Production Managers: Laura Hokkanen, Linda Halls

Page Layout Artist: Danielle Smith
Contributing Editor: Dave Griffin
Technical Consultant: Dave Benner

Working with Drywall
Created by: The Editors of Creative Publishing international, Inc., in cooperation with Black & Decker.
Black & Decker® is a trademark of The Black & Decker Corporation and is used under license.

Contents

Working with Drywall

Introduction

Hanging, taping and finishing drywall are home improvement jobs that everyone dreads. It isn't just that they have a reputation for being messy, awkward, tedious and labor intensive: the majority of people who have installed and finished drywall in their homes have been disappointed by the end result. No matter how thoroughly we sand and how carefully we touch up, most of us never quite manage to achieve a flat, seamless and smooth wall or ceiling surface. So it isn't altogether shocking that many people faced with the task of adding a new wall or ceiling worry about spotty, uneven walls, a touch of back strain and a house full of fine white dust.

It really doesn't need to be that way. Like practically every other DIY chore you'll attempt, getting good drywalling results with minimal effort and mess boils down to choosing the best materials and techniques and then following the directions.

Complete with a bonus CD featuring real-time drywalling action, *Working with Drywall* shows you how to install and finish drywall the professional way. On the pages that follow you will find all the information you need to make smart choices when it comes time to develop a plan and choose tools and materials. Have you ever wondered why some joint compound comes as powder in a bag and other types are sold premixed in a tub? Are there differences that go beyond simple convenience? Is cementboard only used as a tile backer, or does it have other uses? You'll find the answers to these and other questions inside.

Following the chapter on materials and equipment, you will find thorough, step-by-step photos and instructions that focus on marking, cutting and hanging drywall in just about every imaginable residential application—not just walls and ceilings. Wood studs, metal studs, doorways, electrical boxes, lifters, self-feeding screw guns . . . it's all covered in detail.

Once the drywall is hung the fun has just begun. The third chapter in the book presents the fine art of taping and finishing—the part of the process often referred to simply as "mudding". The newest pro-level tools are shown, along with recommended materials and products, presented with clear color photos showing the right technique for each stage of the taping and finishing process. From installing corner bead to sanding joint compound, we cover it all—including professional finishes like stucco veneer and knock-down orange peel texture.

Finally, we demonstrate the techniques used by professionals to create archways, curves, profiled panels, domes and other unique surfaces. Start to finish, it's all here. And don't forget to view the bonus DVD that's included free of charge. In addition to the basics of taping and finishing, you can watch in real time as professional drywaller Dave Benner demonstrates how to apply popular drywall finishes.

Gallery of Drywall Success

These complex architectural forms combine archways and barrel vaults, presenting a drywalling challenge even for professional rockers. Provided the work is done carefully, however, the results will be very impressive.

Built-ins can be installed during the wall construction process, but more often they are scribed and fitted to existing walls.

A neat drywalling job has a clean, professional appearance marked by smooth surfaces. For fans of careful craftsmanship, it is a bit of a shame to conceal such a well-finished drywall installation as this with paint.

Bathroom walls and ceilings can be tricky to work on because the space is so confined and the walls tend to have many boxes and obstructions. Because a bathroom is a damp area, use drywall panels that are designed for damp environments, such as mold-resistant drywall.

A dramatic foyer is created by arching the top of the adjoining hallway ceiling and trimming the door opening with a prefabricated header that follows the curve precisely.

Making large, curved cuts in drywall is much trickier than making straight cuts that usually involve simple scoring and snapping. A drywall saw or spiral saw is necessary to follow the curved lines.

Drywall has a neutral appearance; add texture to support more visually aggressive design motifs, such as a faux-coffered ceiling and an exposed-brick fireplace chase.

The drywall surfaces between the eye-level wainscot panels and the crown molding are every bit as important to the success of these walls as the trimwork. With all the angles and relief areas going on above and below them, these smooth, flawless surfaces are an essential contrast.

Prefabricated domes add high drama to any ceiling, especially when they include a chandelier or an intricate medallion. These days, domes are usually purchased as prefabricated units made from urethane-base materials.

A balcony wall presents an excellent opportunity to use your drywalling skills. The softly curving balcony wall seen here leads the eye up and toward the red wall, which is the focal point of the room. The style is an interesting contrast to the typical formal look we tend to associate with balconies.

Ordinary drywall can take on great interest with a little creativity. Here, flat wood frames are attached to the wall to create the illusion of expensive frame-and-panel wainscoting. The effect is intensified by the use of contrasting paint colors.

Prefabricated archways and columns provide design options for DIYers that only very talented professional plasterers could hope to replicate from scratch.

Windows create an open, expansive feeling that lets in air and light, especially when the windows are installed in large banks. Smooth drywall makes the walls surrounding the windows appear solid and sturdy so the room feels grounded despite all the glass.

Drywalling a multi-story wall beneath a vaulted ceiling requires scaffolding and at least one helper, but the basic hanging and finishing techniques are no different than they are for a standard 8-ft. wall.

This prefabricated wall niche is designed to fit into a wall stud cavity, with no cutting of framing members necessary. The flange on the niche conceals the edges of the opening you'll cut for your drywall, eliminating the need to get a perfect finish on the curved wall cutout.

Repeated arches with slightly differing radii give this partition wall some serious design presence. The arch in the smaller opening over the breakfast bar begins at the same height as the arch in the passageway, so they feel related even though the sizes and shapes differ.

A ceiling medallion provides a transition from the light fixture to the ceiling surface. Some medallions are solid discs while others are made in two half-circular parts so they can be installed without removing the light fixture.

This curved wall executes a half circle that balances nicely with the porthole and bay window in the same room. The curve is gentle enough that it can be created with ½" drywall as long as the front face paper is dampened prior to bending.

Materials & Equipment

A successful drywalling job depends heavily on selecting the best materials and equipment for the task. The process starts with the drywall panels themselves. Not only is choosing the right panel type for your application important to get good results, it can mean the difference between passing a building inspection and having to tear out your work and start over. Contact your local building department early on in the planning stage to get information relevant to your job. Of most concern to building departments are ceilings and firewalls that separate distinct parts of the house—the wall between a house and an attached garage is a typical example—because these areas must meet strict fire code standards.

Another factor to consider when choosing materials is moisture. If the room you're working on is in a high-moisture environment, use panels that resist moisture damage and mold. You may also need special seaming, taping, and mudding products. The information that follows provides a comprehensive guide to help you make these decisions.

Although you can hang drywall using only a hammer and a utility knife, good tools make the job go faster and yield better results. From professional drywall guns with self-feed screws to laser levels, joint compound paddles, and hoppers for applying textured finishes, this chapter provides a comprehensive guide to tools that can be used in any phase of the process.

In this chapter:

- Drywall Panel Types
- Fasteners, Adhesives & Caulks
- Finishing Materials
- Drywall Tools & Equipment

Drywall Panel Types

Up until the 1930s, interior walls were created by troweling wet plaster onto wood or metal lath that had been nailed to the wall framing members. The finished wall required three coats of plaster, each of which had to be permitted to dry or set. The first generation of drywall panels replaced the lath and the heavy "scratch" coat of plaster. Today, even when a traditional plaster wall finish is desired, special blue-papered drywall panels are anchored to the framing to form the base of the wall instead of a hand-troweled scratch coat. This reduces labor and drying time greatly. Since the end of World War II, the typical drywall panel wall requires no finish layer of plaster. Only minor surface corrections are required, including the filling of seams and covering of fastener dimples with joint compound. Eliminating hand-troweled finishes saves time, labor, and money.

Drywall usually consists of a strong paper skin adhered to a gypsum core. The finish-ready face paper wraps around to the back of the panel at the sides, where it overlaps the coarser, more rigid paper used on the back. For handling purposes, sheets of drywall are joined at the ends by removable strips of tape. To facilitate finishing, panels are typically tapered at the long edges. The shallow depression formed where panels meet is easily covered with tape and filled with joint compound for a flat surface that appears continuous. The short, butt-end joints are not recessed and are more challenging to finish.

Drywall is a broad category of building materials that covers many types of panels with various purposes, including common gypsum-based wallcovering panels as well as specialty wallcoverings and tile backers.

Gypsum ▸

Gypsum is a naturally occurring crystal mined from the earth. It is formed when calcium sulfate chemically combines with water. The scrubbers that neutralize sulfuric acid emitted from power plants also create gypsum synthetically. Today much of our gypsum drywall is a byproduct of this effort to protect the environment from acid rain. When buildings burn, the water is driven out of gypsum crystals in drywall, producing steam. This characteristic makes gypsum a fire suppressant, though eventually the dehydrated gypsum will collapse.

Piles of mined gypsum await processing into the basic constituent material used to make drywall.

Types of Panels

Standard drywall is used for most walls and ceilings in dry, interior areas. It comes in 4-ft.-wide panels in lengths ranging from 8 ft. to 16 ft. and in thicknesses of ¼", ⅜", ½", and ⅝". There are also 54"-wide panels for horizontal installations on walls with 9-ft. ceilings.

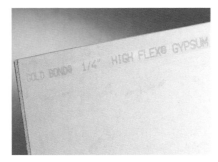

Flexible drywall, specially made for curved walls, is a bendable version of standard ¼"-thick drywall. It can be installed dry or dampened with water to increase its flexibility.

Fire-resistant drywall has a dense, fiber-reinforced core that helps contain fire. Thicknesses are ½", ⅝", and ¾". Most fire-resistant drywall is called "Type X." Fire-resistant panels are generally required in attached garages, on walls adjacent to garages, and in furnace and utility rooms.

Moisture-resistant drywall, commonly called "greenboard" for the color of its face paper, is designed for areas of high-humidity and is used most often in bathrooms, behind kitchen sinks, and in laundry rooms.

Abuse-resistant drywall withstands surface impacts and resists penetrations better than standard drywall. It's available in ½" regular and ⅝" fire-resistant types.

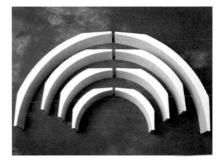

Decorative drywall products include prefinished vinyl-coated panel systems, decorative corner treatments, prefabricated arches, and drywall panels that look like traditional raised-panel paneling.

Sound-resistant drywall products have up to eight times as much sound-deadening capability as standard drywall. These products are good for home theaters.

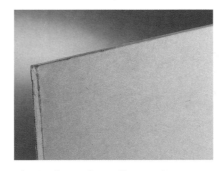

Plaster-base drywall, sometimes called "blueboard," is used with veneer plaster systems instead of a traditional hand-troweled scratch coat. Panels have two layers of paper—a blue-colored face paper that's highly absorptive over a moisture-resistant paper to protect the gypsum core.

Mold-resistant drywall is a specialty board designed for areas that are regularly damp, have high humidity, or that are otherwise susceptible to mold and mildew growth.

Tile Backer ▸

If you're planning to tile new walls in wet areas, such as tub and shower enclosures, use tile backer board as a substrate rather than drywall. Unlike drywall, tile backer won't break down—and ruin the tile job—if water gets behind the tile. There are three basic types of tile backer (see page 156 for supplier information).

Cementboard is made from portland cement and sand reinforced by a continuous outer layer of fiberglass mesh. It's available in $\frac{5}{16}$", $\frac{1}{2}$" and $\frac{5}{8}$" thicknesses. See page 58 to 59 for installation instructions.

Fiber-cement board is similar to cementboard but is somewhat lighter, with fiber reinforcement integrated throughout the panel material. It comes in $\frac{1}{4}$" and $\frac{1}{2}$" thicknesses. Cementboard and fiber-cement board cannot be damaged by water, but water can pass through them. To prevent damage to the framing, install a water barrier of 4-mil plastic or 15# building paper behind the backer.

Dens-Shield®, commonly called glass mat, is a water-resistant gypsum board with a waterproof fiberglass facing. Dens-Shield cuts and installs much like standard drywall but requires galvanized screws to prevent corrosion. Because the front surface provides the water barrier, all untaped joints and penetrations must be sealed with caulk before the tile is installed. Do not use a water barrier behind Dens-Shield.

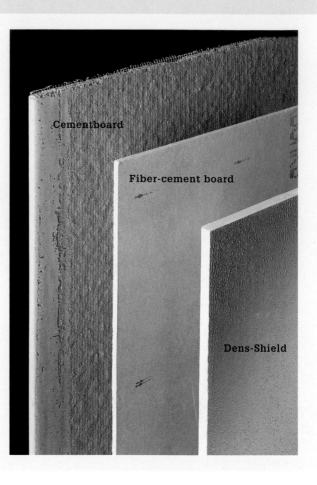

Cementboard

Fiber-cement board

Dens-Shield

Pre-bowing panels helps ensure a tight seal with the framing when using adhesives. The day before installation, stack panels face up, supporting each end with a pair of 2 × 4s. This helps create pressure between the panel and the studs as the memory of the panel tries to revert to the bowed shape.

Using Specialized Drywall Panels

Upgrade to thicker ⅝" panels to achieve greater sag resistance on ceilings with 24" joist spacing or when a finish coat of water-based texture will be applied. The greater thickness also improves fire and sound transmission ratings. Look for Type X drywall.

Flexible ¼" panels can be bent in a tight radius and applied two-layers thick on curved walls. Regular ¼" and ⅜" panels can be attached directly over damaged wall surfaces in remodel and repair work. They also bend well when dampened. The ⅜" panels may also be used in double-layer applications or in a single layer under paneling.

Greenboard panels hold up well under damp conditions in bathrooms, kitchens, and laundry rooms although they do require closer joist spacing on ceilings. The composition of the panel is the same as standard drywall, but the paper is replaced with vinyl facing to repel moisture. For wet areas behind tile, use a tile backerboard like Dens-Shield or cementboard.

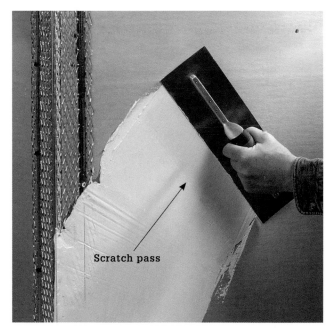

Scratch pass

Plaster-base panels are used when a tough plaster surface is needed to match traditional lath and plaster walls. Plaster-base panels can be attached to the wall or ceiling framing. The special blue paper face allows a strong adhesion with the gypsum plaster while protecting the gypsum core from moisture damage as the plaster dries.

Fasteners, Adhesives & Caulks

Drywall is best fastened with drywall screws—typically black phosphate-coated, coarse-threaded screws that are 1¼" long. Until the rise of the countersinking screwgun, drywall was installed with hammers and ring-shank drywall nails. Nails still have some uses: for example, the initial securing of hard-to-reach portions of wall and ceiling panels. Nails are also often used for securing metal corner bead because they create less distortion of the bead than an over-driven screw. Ring-shank drywall nails should penetrate framing by at least ¾". Nails cannot be used with metal wall studs and framing. Because screws hold drywall more securely than nails, you may employ greater fastener spacing with them (see table on page 47).

Drywall screws are categorized by letters, indicating the type of framing they are best suited to be used with. For wood framing, select Type W screws that penetrate the framing by at least ⅝". For steel framing or to secure gypsum panels to resilient channels, use fine-threaded Type S screws that penetrate the metal by at least ⅜". Use drill-point Type S screws for heavy-gauge steel. To screw gypsum to gypsum in double layers until an adhesive sets, use course threaded Type G screws. Alternatively, use longer Type S or W screws to attach panels to the framing.

Special screws are made for other non-drywall panels. Cementboard is best fastened with cementboard screws that self-tap into the hard cementboard surface and then resist corrosion in the damp, alkaline environment. Use fine threads for steel framing and coarse threads for wood framing. Hot-dipped galvanized roofing nails may also be used to secure cementboard and other tile backers to wood framing.

Some drywall installations also call for the use of adhesives. Ordinary joint compound can function as an adhesive when applied between drywall layers in a two-layer wall. Panel adhesive may be used to laminate drywall panels also. Panel adhesive applied to studs or joists can reduce fastener needs by 75 percent and eliminate the possibility of panels rattling. A spray-on adhesive is used to attach vinyl corner bead to drywall.

Acoustical sealant (caulk) fills openings and cracks that let sound through walls and ceilings and helps isolate drywall panels from the vibration of adjacent surfaces. Used around electric boxes and floor-to-wall seams, it's the least expensive way to improve STC (sound transmission class) ratings. It can also reduce heating and cooling needs by blocking air gaps.

Drywall screws are the fastener of choice for hanging drywall on walls and ceilings, largely because they grip better, are more controllable, and don't pop out like nails can. Many pros still use nails, however, to tack panels into place prior to screwing.

Fastening Drywall Panels

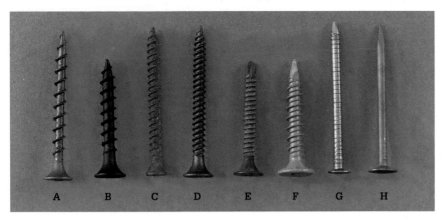

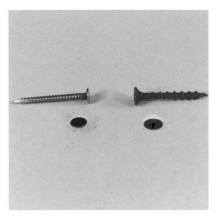

Drywall fasteners include: Type W for screwing panels to wood framing (A); Type G for drawing panels together in multilayer installations (B); Trimhead drywall screws for fastening wood trim to metal studs (C); Type S standard (D) and self-tapping (E) for attaching panels to steel framing; Cementboard screws (F); Ring-shank drywall nails (G); and smooth drywall nails (H).

Drywall screwheads and nail heads are shaped to provide maximum holding power for the panel without tearing the facing paper. Screws have a bugle head that preserves the paper integrity as long as the screw is not overdriven. The undersides of the nail heads have slight, smooth tapers so the heads may be countersunk without tearing through the paper.

Drywall Adhesives ▸

Adhesives can be used in drywall installation, and offer a number of benefits: they create a much stronger bond between framing and panels, they reduce the number of fasteners needed by up to 75 percent, and they can bridge minor irregularities in framing members. There are several types of adhesives and caulks used for installing drywall:

Construction adhesive is used with screws for gluing panels directly to framing or a solid base, such as concrete basement walls.

Panel or laminating adhesive is used for gluing drywall panels to other panels in multi-layer installations, or to bond panels with concrete walls or rigid foam insulation. A few Type G drywall screws may be needed to support panels while the adhesive sets up.

Contact cement is used for attaching other coverings to drywall panels, such as mass loaded vinyl sheeting for soundproofing.

Acoustical sealant, while not an adhesive, is used during multiple layer installations to seal all gaps around the perimeter of installed panels and along corners, ceilings, and floors. Acoustical sealant comes in a tube and is applied with a caulk gun.

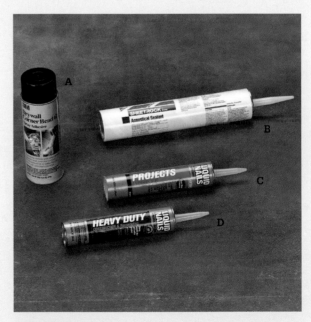

Adhesives useful for installing and finishing drywall include: spray-on adhesive (A) for attaching corner bead; acoustical sealant (B) for filling gaps around panel perimeters in multi-layer installations; panel adhesive (C) and construction adhesive (D) for bonding panels to framing members or other panels.

Finishing Materials

Finishing drywall is the more difficult part of surfacing walls and ceilings, but it's a project well within the ability of a DIY homeowner. Armed with a basic understanding of the variety of finish materials available, you'll be able to walk out of your local home center or drywall supplier with the exact supplies you need to cover all joints, corners and fasteners for a successful drywall project.

The primary materials used in finishing are corner bead, tape, and joint compound. Corner bead is the angle strip—usually made of metal or vinyl—that covers a drywall corner, creating a straight, durable edge where walls intersect. Joint tape is combined with joint compound to create a permanent layer that covers the drywall seams, as well as small holes and gaps. Without tape, thick applications of compound are highly prone to cracking. There are two types of joint tape: paper and self-adhesive fiberglass mesh. Joint compound, commonly called "mud," seals and levels all seams, corners, and depressions in a drywall installation. It's also used for skim coating and some texturing treatments. There are several types of compounds, with important differences among them, but the two main forms are used for setting and drying (setting-type and drying-type).

Materials for finishing your drywall-coated wall include: bead and tape (for covering corners and seams), joint compound (for covering dimples, dents, bead and tape) and texturing materials (for creating a spray-texture surface).

Estimating Materials ▶

The following tips will help you determine how much of each material you will need for your project. Add 10 to 15 percent to your estimate to cover waste and mistakes.

Corner Bead: Count the number of corners and the lengths of each, and purchase enough bead to cover each in one piece. Beads are available in standard lengths of 8 to 10 ft.

Joint Tape: Approximately 375 ft. of tape will finish 1000 sq. ft. of drywall.

Compound: The following are estimates. Check with the manufacturer for actual coverage information. For every 100 sq. ft. of drywall, you'll need approximately:

*   1 gallon of pre-mixed, drying-type compound (taping, topping, and all purpose)
*   8 lbs. of powder drying-type compound
*   7½ lbs. of standard powder setting-type compound
*   5½ lbs. of lightweight powder setting-type compound

Corner Bead

Corners, seams, and edges of drywall should not be left unprotected. Instead, apply preformed corner strips (called *bead*) or pre-seamed tape to make a crisp edge and protect the drywall from damage. A 90° inside corner is usually finished with drywall joint tape, but outside and off-angle inside corners are best finished with corner beads.

Metal corner bead is a rigid, tough corner bead that's installed with drywall nails or screws driven through the drywall and into the framing. It also may be installed with a crimping tool.

Vinyl outside corner bead is applied with staples or a spray-on adhesive.

Paper-faced metal or plastic corner bead is embedded in joint compound on outside corners. No fasteners are needed but a special roller tool is recommended to bed the legs properly.

Off-angle corner bead makes inside and outside corners greater than 90° much easier to finish. Off-angle corner bead comes in rolls or straight lengths and features a flexible center. Some have a raised ridge that, when facing out, may be used for outside corners. Others have a rubberized center to allow for movement as the house settles.

Bullnose outside-corner bead and inner-cove bead leave a curved corner. Outside bullnose corners require that the drywall not overlap at the corner to leave room for the radius corner.

Corner bead for arches has one edge cut into segments for bending along an arch.

J-bead and L-bead are attached to the edges of drywall that are left open or that meet a non-drywall surface, such as wood or brick. J-bead must be installed before the drywall panel is fastened at the finished edge. L-bead may come with a tear-away masking strip to protect adjacent surfaces while finishing.

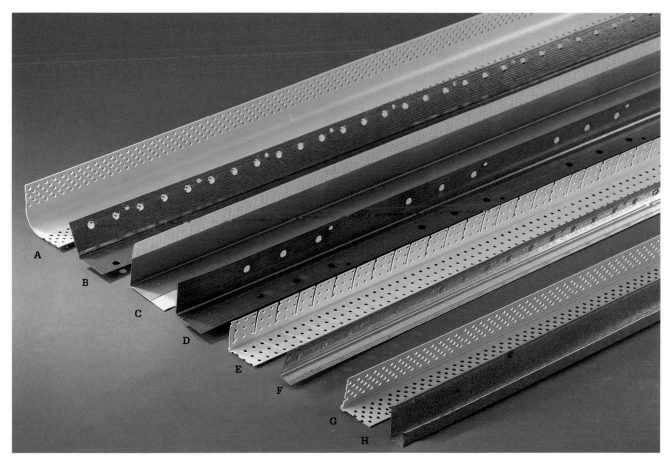

Corner bead options include: bullnose and inner-cove corner beads (A); off-angle corner beads for inside or outside corners (B); paper-faced metal or plastic outside corner bead (C); metal outside corner bead (D); corner bead for arches (E); L-bead (F); vinyl outside corner bead (G); and J-bead (H).

Joint Tape & Compound

Made of paper or fiberglass mesh, joint tape is sold in rolls usually 75 or 150 ft. long. Paper tape makes crisper inside corners because it is pre-creased lengthwise. It is also resistant to accidental cutting with a taping knife. The self-adhesive, fiberglass-mesh tape applies easily to flat joints and does not need to be set into a joint compound bed (whereas paper tape must be). Fiberglass mesh tape works better for making quick repairs.

Joint compound is used as both a bonding agent and filler. It goes on smoothly, dries hard, and sands easily (albeit with much dust). It is sold in two forms: as a dry powder in a bag and as a premixed compound in a tub. Setting-type (powder) joint compounds are mixed with water on site. It sets stronger, harder and faster than pre-mixed compounds and it doesn't shrink as much. Setting-type compounds are best mixed with a mixing paddle used with a power drill. It is important that the blend be well-mixed, as any lumps will affect the finished surface and make it very difficult to smooth out the mud. Unlike premixed compound, setting-type compound hardens in the bucket if it sits longer than the set time, and even "easy sand" varieties resist sanding more than drying-type compounds. Set times of compounds vary from forty-five minutes to as much as six hours. They harden by chemical reaction.

Drying-type joint compounds come premixed in one- and five-gallon tubs. They set by drying and are not as strong or fast-setting as setting-type compounds. Drying-type joint compounds come in taping, topping, and all-purpose formulas. Advantages to drying-type compounds include convenience, ability to save leftover compound for months and ease of sanding. Use topping compound for second and third coats only. Lightweight, all-purpose joint compound may be used for both taping and topping when convenience dictates.

Joint tape comes in two primary types: pre-creased paper tape that can be used on inside corners, outside corners or flat seams, and self-adhesive fiberglass mesh, which is best suited for flat seams and repairs.

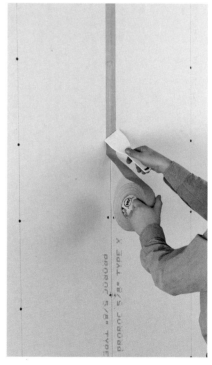

Fire-rated tape is another convenient self-adhesive tape, used for surfaces that are finished just enough to meet fire codes. It doesn't need a coat of compound to achieve its fire rating. It is a popular choice in attached garages where common walls between the garage and house must meet fire-rating standards.

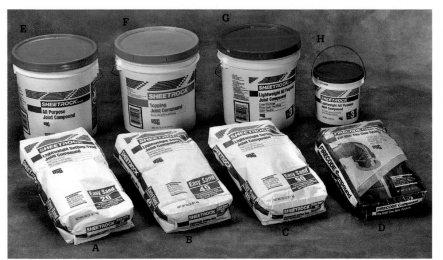

Drywall joint compounds include: setting-type joint compounds in 20-minute, 45-minute and 90-minute grades (A, B, C); fireproof taping compound (D); premixed all-purpose joint compound (E); premixed topping compound (F); premixed lightweight all-purpose compound (G, H).

Texturing Materials ▸

Texturing mud can be ready-mix topping compound or specially designed for the look you are trying to achieve. Texturing compounds often come in dry powder form and are blended with water using a hand mixer or a drill and paddle.

Aggregated ceiling textures have coarse to fine aggregates like polystyrene or perlite particles already mixed in to achieve popcorn or cottage cheese texture and other rough surfaces.

Orange peel and knock down textures are for walls and ceilings. The effects are produced with smooth (unaggregated) compound, such as lightweight, all-purpose joint compound.

Acoustical textures, used for ceilings and other non-contact surfaces, are made from a compound designed to absorb sound.

Texturing mud is applied to walls and ceilings with pneumatic spray equipment, such as a hopper gun, which can be rented along with an air compressor to drive the sprayer. Texture may also be applied with a long-handled paint roller. When mixed to a thicker consistency, texturing mud may be applied like joint compound using finishing trowels or knives.

Adjacent finished surfaces need to be protected diligently when texturing. A paper roller that lays 12" masking paper with masking tape along one edge comes in very handy, as does a spray shield. Use a knock-down knife to flatten the peaks when creating a knock-down texture. A 12" knife can also be used, though it may leave edge tracks. Any number of brushes can be used to stipple or swirl compound into interesting textures.

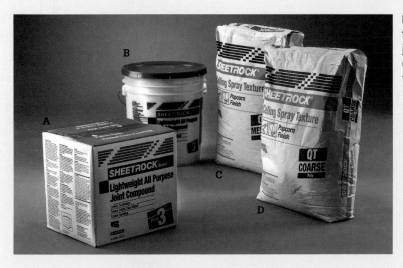

Products for applying textured finishes include: lightweight pre-mixed joint-compound (A, B); medium aggregate ceiling texture (C); coarse aggregate ceiling texture (D).

Drywall Tools & Equipment

To hang drywall, you'll need a variety of tools to measure, mark and cut panels to size, as well as fasten them to the framing. A tape measure is a necessity for measuring and marking drywall—a 25-footer is a versatile choice. A T-square saves time by helping you make straight, square cuts across the entire width of a panel; a chalk line creates layout and cutting lines across greater spans. To check the framing for plumb and square, a framing square and four-foot level are handy.

The principal tool for cutting drywall is a utility knife. Make sure you have plenty of fresh blades on hand, swapping out the dull ones often. Use a drywall rasp to smooth cut panel edges. A standard compass is necessary for scribing adjacent surfaces onto a panel and creating small circles for cutouts. For larger circles, use a drywall compass to score the panel. A drill can also be outfitted with a hole saw for pipes and other small round cutouts. A keyhole saw makes quick work of small holes, such as those for electrical boxes. A drywall saw quickly cuts notches for doors, windows, and other openings. For faster speed in making cutouts, use a spiral saw to cut through panels after they have been installed.

The best tool for hanging drywall is a screw gun. Similar to a drill, a screw gun has an adjustable clutch that stops driving the screw at a preset depth. For large jobs, it's practical to rent a screw gun; otherwise, use a variable speed ⅜" drill with a dimpling tool and carefully drive the screws. A drywall lifter helps you prop up panels while fastening them, but a flat bar can perform the same function. Apply adhesives and caulking using a caulk gun.

Drywall hand tools can be purchased at home centers at reasonable prices. If you don't wish to buy power tools, most of them can be found at rental centers, along with a variety of specialty tools. During every phase of a drywall project, make sure to protect yourself from the dust and debris generated—always wear protective eyewear and a dust mask or respirator, especially when sanding.

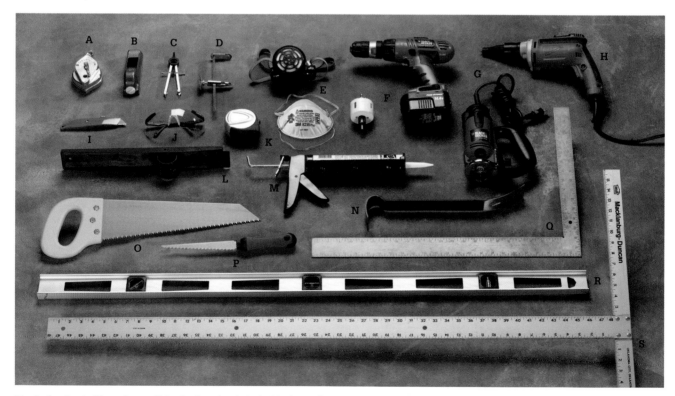

Tools for installing drywall include: plumb bob (A), drywall rasp (B), compass (C), drywall compass (D), protective masks (E), drill with hole saw (F), spiral saw (G), drywall gun (H), utility knife (I), eye protection (J), tape measure (K), drywall lifter (L), caulk gun (M), pry bar (N), drywall saw (O), keyhole saw (P), framing square (Q), level (R), drywall T-square (S).

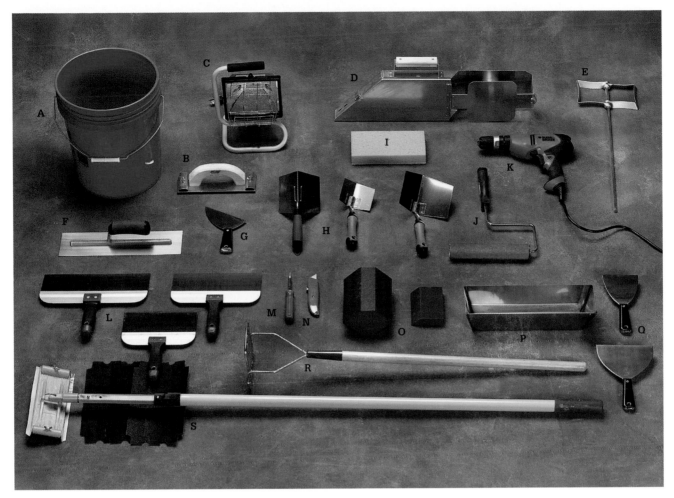

Drywall finishing tools include: 5-gallon bucket (A); hand/block sander (B); work light (C); drywall banjo (D); mixing paddle (E); 12" finishing trowel (F); 6" angled taping knife (G); corner taping knives (H); wet sanding sponge (I); paint roller with tight-nap roller cover (J); ½" drill (K); taping knives (8", 10", 12") (L); screwdriver (M); utility knife (N); dry sanding sponges (O); mud pan (P); taping knives (4", 6") (Q); hand masher (R); 120-, 150-, 220-grit sanding screens, sandpaper and pole sander (S).

A successful drywall finish job is one that isn't seen once the paint or wallcovering is applied. A flawless finish is a lot easier to obtain when you use the proper tools for the job. Mixing joint compound with a ½" heavy-duty drill and a mixing paddle, for example, yields superior product and takes far less time than mixing by hand (although using a hand masher will improve your results). Another useful tool is a mud pan that holds the compound while you work. It fits nicely into your hand and has sharp edges for scraping excess mud from taping knives.

As for knives, the minimum you'll need are a 6" knife for taping and a 12" knife for the filler and final coats—though a 4" taping knife is handy for tight spots, and some prefer a 10" knife for the filler coat. There are a number of specialty knives available that can help make taping easier, such as a double-bladed knife for inside corners and angled knives for tight spots. Many

drywall installers also find a 12" finishing trowel handy for feathering the final coat. Don't buy bottom-line or plastic knives, even for a small job—the money saved won't justify the frustration.

Sanding completes the job. Professionals use a pole sander with replaceable fiberglass sanding screens—a versatile and effective tool, and quite handy for ceilings. For hand sanding, sanding blocks and dry sanding sponges will take care of the finish work, and a bright work light can help draw attention to overlooked areas.

If you will be skim-coating surfaces, you'll also need a 5-gallon bucket for thinning down compound and a paint roller with a tight-nap roller cover for application. Finally, keep a few general tools on hand for making adjustments as you work, such as a utility knife for trimming tape or panels at butt joints, and a screwdriver to drive protruding heads.

Specialty Tools

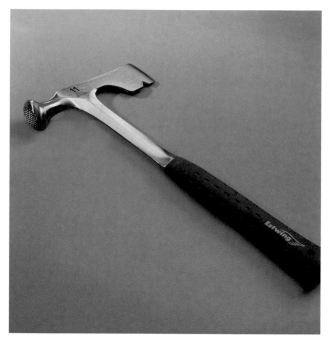

A drywall hammer has a textured face that creates indented lines in the paper without breaking the surface. The lines create tooth to help joint compound bond to the drywall surface. The claw end of a drywall hammer is flattened to function as a pry bar to jack panels into place.

A panel carrier supports drywall panels from below and includes a carrying handle so panels can be easily carried by one person.

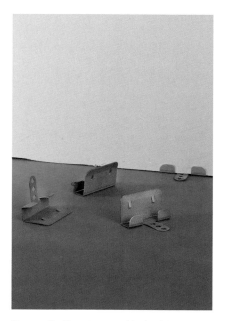

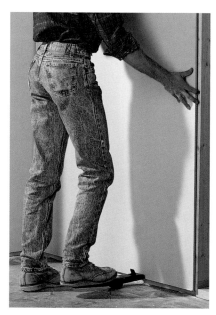

Drywall stilts are a useful way to reach the ceiling and retain mobility. Use them only for finishing drywall and only after the room has been cleared of debris and drop cloths. Do not use them when installing drywall panels—it is a very dangerous practice.

Drywall clips are used to isolate corner joints from the movement of adjacent framing members. They also facilitate optimal thermal insulation of walls by reducing the number of studs and backers needed.

A drywall lifter is basically a one piece metal lever that slips underneath the panel at floor level. Stepping on the lift pedal causes the panel to rise about ½", which is the recommended minimum gap between the floor and the bottom of the panel.

Drywall benches have broad bench tops so they can be used as step stools as well as sawhorses for holding panels to be cut. Most are adjustable for ideal access to upper walls and ceilings.

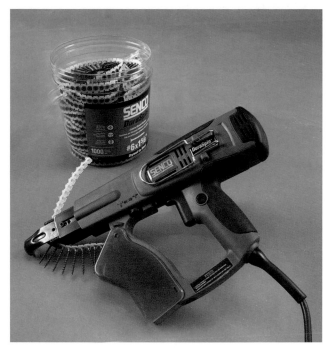

Drywall guns feature a special chuck for automatic depth control of the screw head. Self-feeding models automatically load drywall screws collated on plastic strips, saving time. If you do not use self-feeding guns regularly, calibrating them can be tricky. Also, the cost-per-screw is much higher. They can be rented at most building or rental centers.

A panel lift is a rented tool that allows you to lift drywall to a ceiling or high wall. It is stable and will hold the panel as long as necessary, making it an indispensable tool if you will be working alone.

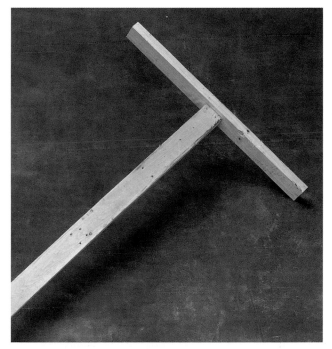

A pair of T-braces or "deadmen" that are 1" taller than the ceiling height can help hold drywall against the framing during ceiling installations. Cut a straight 2 × 4 so it's ½" shorter than the ceiling height, then fasten a 36"-long 2 × 4 to the end for the bracing arm.

(continued)

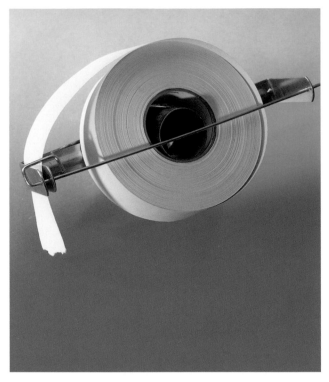

A drywall tape reel holds 500-ft.-long rolls of paper joint tape and clips to a belt for easy access. It includes a threaded slot for easy tear-off.

A drywall hawk can be loaded with joint compound and toted around so you can take just as much as you need for each dimple or seam.

A drywall banjo is a relatively inexpensive taping machine that passes paper tape through a box filled with thinned joint compound for simultaneous tape and mud application. These also can be rented at larger rental centers.

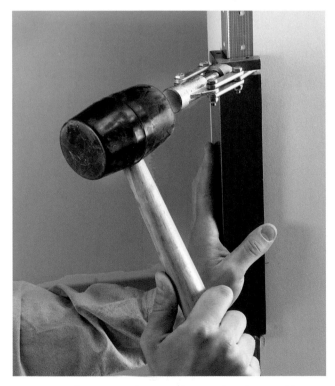

A corner crimper attaches metal corner bead to outside corners without the use of fasteners. It's especially useful for metal-framed walls where nails don't grip.

Sanding systems can reduce airborne dust by up to 95%. Most systems are available with both pole and hand sanding attachments that connect to a wet/dry vacuum. Water filters are also available for catching dust before it reaches the vacuum.

Air compressors and sprayguns with handheld hoppers are used to apply texture to walls and ceilings, and are available for rent. While they are relatively easy to use, get an operator's manual or lesson at the rental center, then practice on a scrap of cardboard before attempting your project.

Cleaning Drywall Finishing Tools ▶

Taping tools can be cleaned easily with water. Rinse and wipe off taping knives, mud pans, and mixing paddles immediately after use. Do not clean tools in a sink—compound can settle in pipes where it will harden and clog drains. Wipe down and dry tools thoroughly to prevent rust.

Hang taping knives to store them so the blades will not be bent or damaged by other tools. A pegboard hanger system is perfect for this task, and the knives will be easy to locate when you need them.

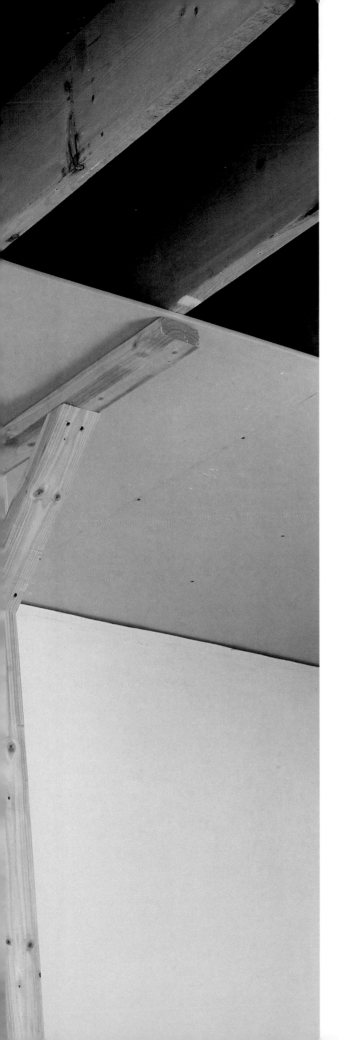

Drywall Installation

Hanging drywall panels can be an awkward task marked by heavy lifting and strenuous physical feats. Or it can be an efficient process that exploits the mechanical advantages of specialized drywall tools and accessories. Unless you are counting on home improvement work for exercise and conditioning, the recommendations in this chapter will help take the pain and frustration out of the drywalling process.

As a general rule, use the smallest number of drywall panels possible to minimize seams and potential cracks. Unfortunately, bigger panels are heavier, which is a particular issue when you're drywalling a ceiling. If you have ever tried to hold a full sheet of ⅝" drywall overhead for several minutes while someone else fumbles to get a screw in place, you can probably still feel the strain in your arms and shoulders. Instead, use a drywall lift (page 49)—a miraculous rental tool that does the heavy lifting for you.

A little knowledge will go a long way toward helping you measure and cut accurately. You can also save time by choosing the right fasteners and adjusting the clutch for just the right amount of countersink. Get these small details right and you can complete the biggest job much faster.

In this chapter:

Making a Layout Plan

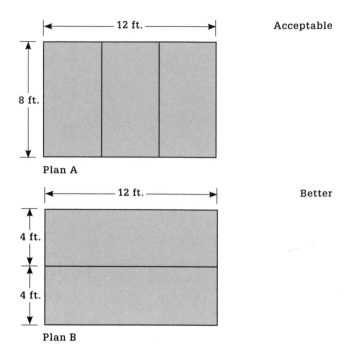

Planning the layout of drywall panels prior to installation makes it a lot easier to create a materials list, minimize seams and solve potential problems before they crop up. Take careful measurements and sketch each wall and ceiling to be covered. Note the center-to-center (O.C.) spacing of the framing members, which can determine the thickness of drywall you install as well as how you install it (either parallel or perpendicular to the framing). See the chart on the opposite page for maximum framing spacing allowances.

Standard drywall is commonly available in widths of 4 feet and 54" and lengths of 8, 10, 12, 14, and 16 feet. It's in your best interest to use the longest drywall panels you can: it'll save you a lot of work during the finishing phase. Home centers and lumberyards always have 4 × 8 foot panels in stock and usually carry smaller quantities of the other sizes, or you can special order them.

The goal of planning the optimal drywall layout is to minimize seams. Seams require joint tape, compound and sanding, which means the less of them there are, the less work you have ahead of you. For wall or ceiling surfaces 48" wide or less, cover the entire area using a single drywall panel. With no seams to tape, you'll only have to cover the screw heads with a few thin coats of compound.

Walls that are wider than 48" will require at least two panels. While there are a number of ways you can hang them, some possibilities yield better results than others. For example, for a wall that is 8 feet high and 12 feet long (as shown in first two plans at the top right), three panels could be installed vertically (Plan A), resulting in only tapered seams and no butt joints. However, this plan requires 16 linear feet of vertical taping, working from floor to ceiling, which is more difficult than taping a horizontal seam. Using two 4 × 12 feet panels (Plan B) reduces the amount of taping by 25 percent and places the seam about waist high, easing the finishing process. While a reduction of 25 percent of the finish work may not mean much on a small project, on a large remodel or new construction it can save you a lot of time and money.

Avoid butt joints where possible, but if they are necessary, locate them as far from the center of the wall as possible to help mask the seam. While it is best to use full panels, do not butt a tapered edge to panel ends (Plan C). This configuration produces an

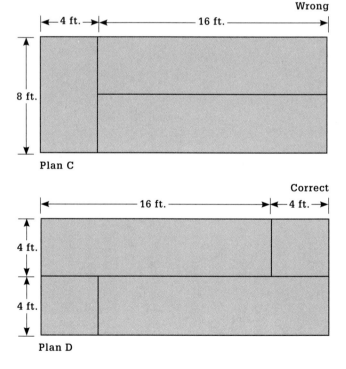

8-ft. long butt seam that will be difficult to finish. The best solution is to stagger the long panels and fill in with pieces cut from another (Plan D). For all butt joints, panel ends must break on a framing member unless you plan to use back blocking to recess the seam (see page 57).

In rooms with ceilings over 8 feet in height, use 54"-wide panels. If ceilings are taller than 9 feet, consider using longer panels installed vertically.

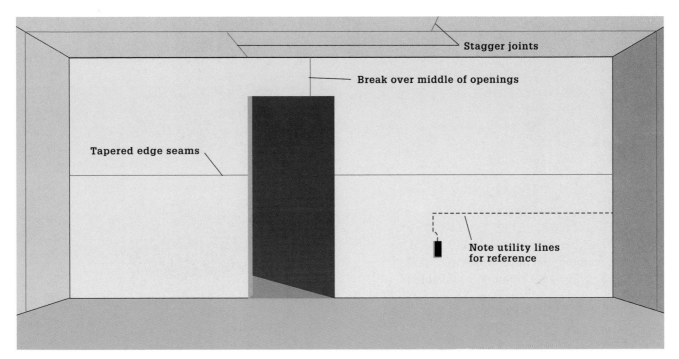

Drywall seams must fall on the centers of framing members, so measure and mark the framing when planning your layout. Use long sheets horizontally to span an entire wall. Avoid butted end joints whenever possible; where they do occur, stagger them between rows so they don't fall on the same framing member. Don't place seams over the corners of doors, windows or other openings—joints there often crack or cause bulges that interfere with trim. Where framing contains utility lines, draw a map for future reference, noting locations of wiring,a pipes and shutoff valves.

Maximum Framing Spacing ▸

Panel Thickness	Installation	Maximum Framing Spacing
⅜"	Ceilings, perpendicular to Framing	16" O.C.
	Walls	16" O.C.
½"	Ceilings, parallel to Framing	16" O.C.
	Ceilings, perpendicular to Framing	24" O.C.
	Walls	24" O.C.
⅝"	Ceilings, parallel to Framing	16" O.C.
	Ceilings, perpendicular to Framing	24" O.C.
	Walls	24" O.C.

▌Estimating Materials

To estimate the number of drywall panels you'll need, simply count the number used in your layout sketch. For larger projects, you can do a quick estimation for 4 × 8 foot panels by measuring the length of the walls and dividing the total by 4. For each window, subtract a quarter panel; for doors, half a panel. Keep in mind that panels are sold in pairs, so round odd numbered totals up to an even number.

The number of screws you'll need depends on the spacing of your framing and the fastener spacing schedule required (see page 47). For a rough estimate, calculate the square footage of the wall and ceiling surfaces and multiply by one fastener per square foot. Drywall screws are sold in pounds—one pound of screws equals roughly 320 screws. Construction adhesive is available in tubes. Check the manufacturer's specifications on the tube for coverage.

Preparing for Drywall Installation

Begin your installation project by checking the framing—and adding blocking, if necessary—and planning the layout of the panels. Minor flaws in the framing can be hidden by the drywall and joint compound, but a severely bowed or twisted stud or crowned or sagging joists will result in an uneven finished surface.

Check the framing using your eye, a straight board, or a string. Bad studs or joists can be planed down, furred out, or replaced, but for serious ceiling problems it's sometimes easiest to add a grid of furring strips or install a steel channel ceiling system (see page 39).

Following your layout plan, measure and mark the location of seams to ensure there is adequate backing for panels. Install 2× blocking where needed to provide additional fastening support.

Tools & Materials ▸

Work gloves
Eye protection
Hammer
Tape measure
Framing square
Handsaw
Plane
Screwgun or drill
2× framing lumber

10d framing nails
Wood shims
Drywall screws
Metal protector plates
Foam insulation
Furring strips
Cardboard strips
Stapler

Drywall Preparation

Install protector plates where wires or pipes pass through framing members and are less than 1¼" from the front edge. The plates keep drywall screws from puncturing wires or pipes.

Wrap water pipes along the ceiling with foam insulation before covering them with drywall. This prevents condensation on the pipes that can drip onto the drywall and cause staining.

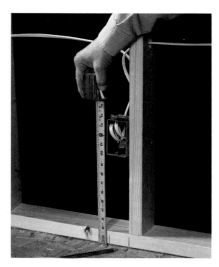

Mark the location and dimensions of electrical boxes on the floor. This makes it easier to locate them during drywall installation.

Installing Blocking

Add backing to support panel edges that don't fall over framing. When installing new panels next to an existing wall surface, or where the framing layout doesn't coincide with the drywall edges, it's often easiest to add an extra stud for backing.

Add crossblocking with 24" O.C. spacing between framing members where needed to help support edges of drywall panels at joints.

Fasten 2 × 4 nailers to the top plate of walls that run parallel to joists. This provides a fastening surface for ceiling panels. The nailer should overhang the plate by half its width.

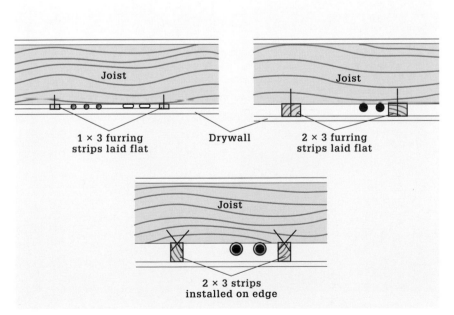

Joist

1 × 3 furring
strips laid flat

Drywall

Joist

2 × 3 furring
strips laid flat

Joist

2 × 3 strips
installed on edge

Attach furring strips where service lines and other obstacles project beyond the framing. The strips create a flat surface for attaching drywall and can also be used to compensate for uneven joists. Use 1 × 3 or 2 × 3 furring strips and attach them perpendicularly to the framing with drywall screws. Space the strips 16" O.C. and use wood shims secured behind the strips to adjust for unevenness.

Use plywood strips to join panel edges in problem areas between framing, creating a floating seam. This method does not provide a substitute for structural backing; the panels still must be supported by framing or blocking.

Straightening Bowed Studs

Use a long, straight 2 × 4 as a guide to check the alignment of studs. Hold the 2 × 4 against the studs both horizontally and diagonally, looking for gaps. To check a corner for square, use a 24" framing square.

For studs that bow outward slightly, use a plane or chisel to trim the facing edge just enough so it is flush with the surrounding framing.

Studs in nonload-bearing walls bowed inward more than ¼" can be straightened. Using a handsaw, make a 2" cut into the stud at the midpoint of the bow. Pull the stud outward, and glue a tapered wood shim into the saw cut to hold the stud straight. Attach a 2-ft.-long 2 × 4 brace to one side of the stud to strengthen it, then trim off the shim. Replace any studs that are severely twisted.

Staple cardboard strips to stud faces. Use solid strips (not corrugated), which are available from drywall suppliers, or mat board from an art supply store. For extreme bows, start with a 12 to 24" strip and add layers of successively longer strips.

Installing a Suspended Ceiling System for Drywall

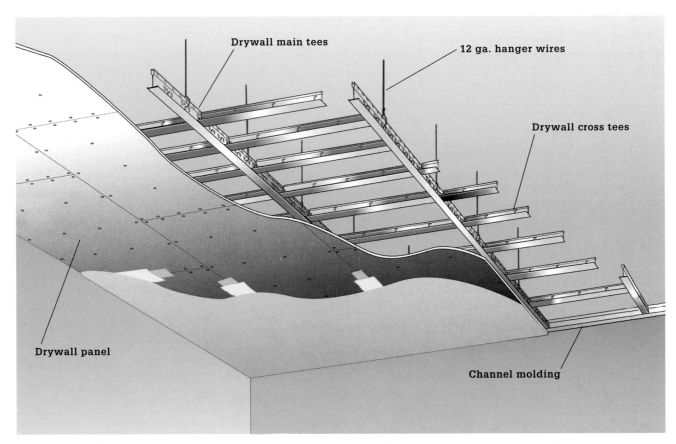

Drywall main tees

12 ga. hanger wires

Drywall cross tees

Drywall panel

Channel molding

Suspended ceiling systems for drywall are installed similarly to suspended acoustical ceilings. The resilient steel tees, channels, and heavy-gauge wire work together to create a base grid strong enough to support up to two layers of ⅝" fire-rated drywall. Like steel framing, steel channels and tees can be cut to length using aviation snips or a saw outfitted with a metal cutting blade. Once the ceiling system is in place, drywall panels are installed as in a conventional installation. For ½" and ⅝" panels, use 1" Type S (fine thread) drywall screws.

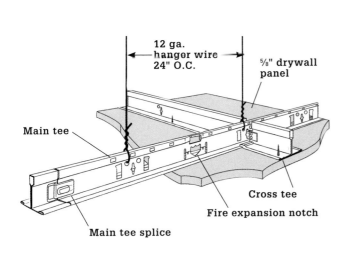

12 ga. hanger wire 24" O.C.

⅝" drywall panel

Main tee

Cross tee

Fire expansion notch

Main tee splice

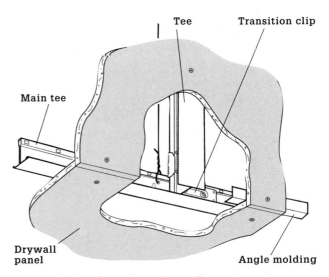

Tee

Transition clip

Main tee

Drywall panel

Angle molding

Main tees should be supported every 24" O.C. for ½" and ⅝" ceiling panels, and a maximum of 16" O.C. for thicker panels. Use 12-gauge hanger wires fastened to the ceiling joists. Fasten the channel molding to framing members with 1¼" drywall screws.

Form vertical surfaces for ceiling soffits or ductwork raceways by screwing drywall panels to tees that are attached to the main tees with transition clips.

Measuring & Cutting Drywall

Drywall is one of the easiest building materials to install, partly because it allows for minor errors. Most professionals measure and cut to the nearest ⅛", and it's perfectly acceptable to trim off a little extra from a panel to make it easier to get into a tight space. The exceptions to this are cutouts for electrical boxes and recessed light fixtures, which must be accurate, because the coverplates usually hide less then you think they will.

Make sure your utility knife is sharp. A sharp blade ensures clean, accurate cuts that slice through the face paper and score the gypsum core in one pass. A dull blade can slip from the cutting line to snag and rip the face paper and is more likely to cause injury.

With a sharp utility knife, you can make cuts from either side of panels. But when using drywall and keyhole saws, make all cuts from the front side to prevent tearing the face paper. For projects that require a number of cutouts, use a spiral saw. This tool makes short work of large openings and electrical boxes, though it generates a lot of dust, so make sure to wear a dust mask. Inexpensive spiral saws are available at home centers, or you can use a standard router outfitted with a piloted drywall bit.

Tools & Materials ▸

Work gloves	Keyhole saw
Eye protection	Compass or
Tape measure	drywall compass
T-square	Spiral saw
Pencil	Drywall panels
Chalkline	Clamps
Utility knife	Straightedge
Drywall rasp	Chalk
Drywall saw	

How to Make Straight Cuts

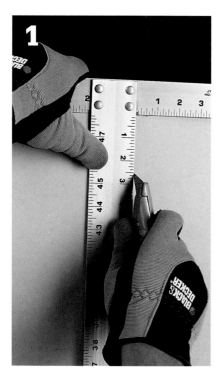

Mark the length on the face of the panel, then set a T-square at the mark. Hold the square in place with your hand and foot and cut through the face paper using a utility knife with sharp blade.

Bend the scored section backward with both hands to snap the gypsum core.

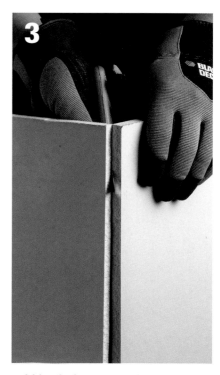

Fold back the waste piece and cut through the back paper with the utility knife.

How to Make Angled Cuts

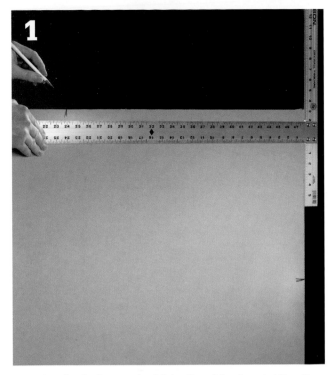

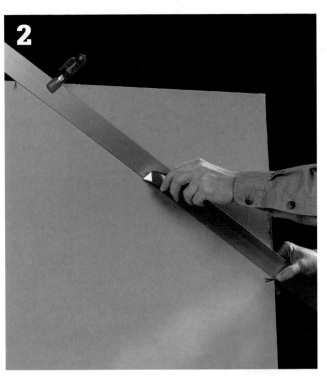

Measure both the vertical "rise" and horizontal "run" of the area and mark the dimensions along the corresponding edges of the panel.

Connect the marks with a T-square, hold down firmly, and score the drywall from point to point. Finish the cut using the "snap cut" method on page 40; be careful not to damage the pointed ends.

Making Rough Cuts ▶

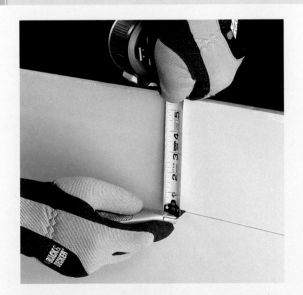

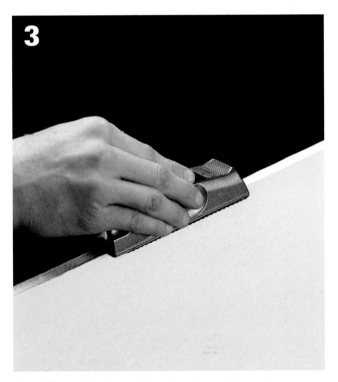

Make horizontal cuts using a tape measure and utility knife. With one hand, hold the knife blade at the end of the tape. With the other hand, grip the tape at the desired measurement—slide this hand along the panel edge as you make the cut.

Smooth rough edges with a drywall rasp. One or two passes with the rasp should be sufficient. To help fit a piece into a tight space, bevel the edge slightly toward the back of the panel.

How to Cut Notches

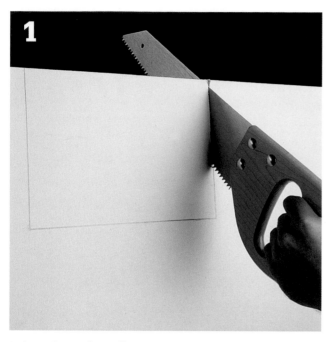

Using a large drywall saw, cut the vertical sides of the notch. (These saws are also handy for cutting out door and window openings after the drywall is installed.)

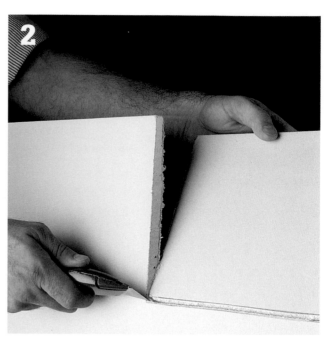

Cut the face paper along the bottom of the notch using a utility knife. Snap the waste piece backward to break the core, then cut through the back paper.

How to Cut Large Openings

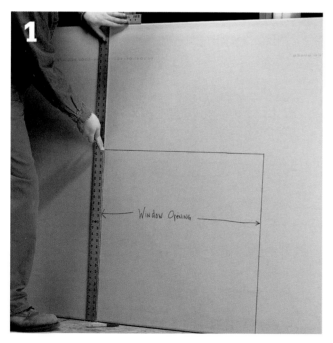

Measure the location of the cutout and transfer the dimensions to the backside of the panel. Score along the line that represents the header of the opening using a straightedge and utility knife.

Install the panel over the opening. The scored line should fall at the header. Cut the drywall along the jambs and up to the header using a drywall saw. Snap forward the waste piece to break the core, then cut through the face paper and remove.

How to Cut an Electrical Box Opening: Coordinate Method

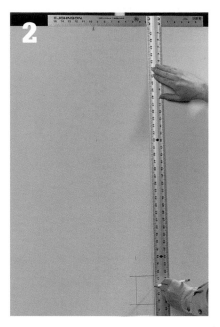

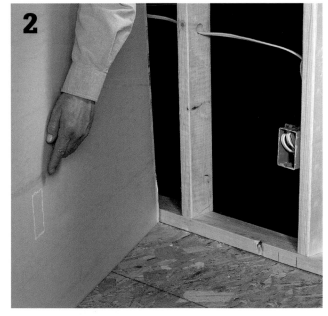

Locate the four corners of the box by measuring from the nearest fixed edge—a corner, the ceiling, or the edge of an installed panel—to the outside edges of the box.

Transfer the coordinates to the panel and connect the points, using a T-square. Measure from the panel edge that will abut the fixed edge you measured from. If the panel has been cut short for a better fit, make sure to account for this in your measurements.

Drill a pilot hole in one corner of the outline, then make the cutout with a keyhole saw.

How to Cut an Electrical Box Opening: Chalk Method

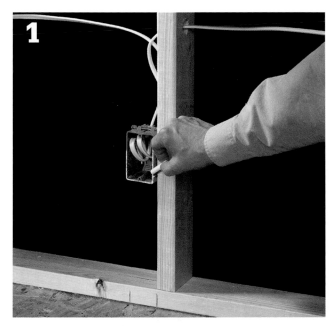

Rub the face of the electrical box with chalk, then position the panel where it will be installed, and press it into the box.

Pull the panel back from the wall; a chalk outline of the box is on the back of the panel. Drill a pilot hole in one corner of the outline, then make the cut with a keyhole saw.

How to Cut Round Holes in Drywall

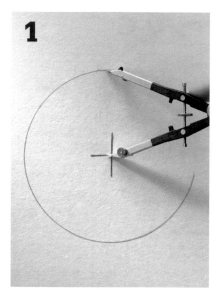
1

To make round cutouts, measure to the center of the object, then transfer the centerpoint to the drywall panel. Use a compass set to half the diameter of the cutout to mark the circle on the panel face.

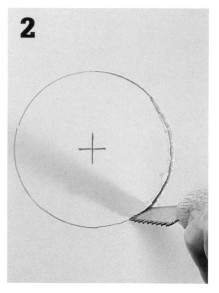
2

Force the pointed end of a drywall saw through the panel from the face side, then saw along the marked line. (These saws work well for all internal cuts.)

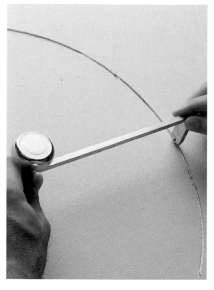

Variation: Drive the point of a drywall compass into the center marking, then rotate the compass wheel to cut the face paper. Tap a nail through the centerpoint, score the back paper, then knock out the hole through the face.

How to Make a Cutout for a Round Fixture Box

1

Locate the four outermost edges of the round box by measuring from the nearest fixed edge—a corner, the ceiling, or the edge of an installed panel—to the outermost edges of the box.

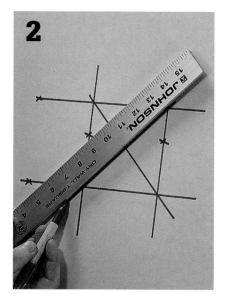
2

Transfer the coordinates to the panel, measuring from the panel edge that will abut the fixed edge you measured from, then connect the points using a T-square. The point where the lines intersect is the centerpoint of the circle. *Note: If the panel has been cut short for a better fit, make sure to account for this in your measurements.*

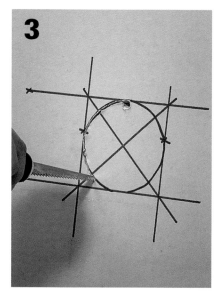
3

Use a compass to draw the outline of the round box on the panel (see above). Drill a pilot hole at one point of the outline, then make the cutout with a keyhole saw. *Note: To avoid the need for a stainblocker, substitute a pencil for a permanent marker.*

Making Cuts with a Compass

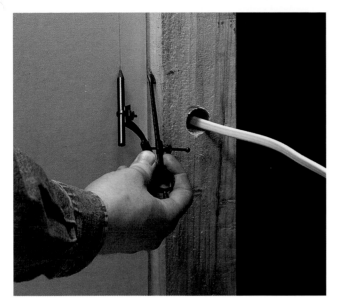

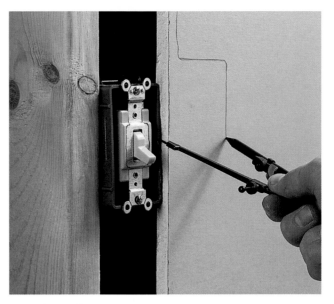

For out-of-square corners, cut the panel 1" longer than necessary, then hold it in position so it is plumb. Set a compass at 1¼", then run it along the wall to scribe the corner onto the face of the panel. Snap cut along the line using a utility knife (see page 40).

Irregular surfaces can be scribed onto panels using the same method. Cut along the scribe line with a keyhole saw, then test fit the piece and make adjustments as necessary.

Cutting Drywall with a Spiral Saw

Spiral saws (or drywall routers) are handy for cutting holes for electrical boxes and openings. You can use a spiral saw made for the purpose or outfit a standard router by removing the router base and installing a piloted drywall bit.

For electrical boxes, mark the floor at the locations of the box centers. Hang the drywall, fastening only at the top edge. Plunge the bit into the box center, move the bit sideways to the edge, then carefully work the bit to the outside. Follow the outside of the box, cutting counterclockwise.

For doorways and other openings, install the drywall over the opening. Moving clockwise, let the bit follow the inside of the frame to make the cutout. Always work clockwise when cutting along the inside of a frame; counterclockwise when following the outside of an object, like an electrical box.

Fastening Drywall

The key to fastening drywall is to countersink screwheads to create a slight recess, or "dimple," without breaking the face paper. The best tool for the job is a screwgun, which has an adjustable clutch that can be set to stop screws at a preset depth. A variable speed drill/driver and a light touch will also get the job done.

When driving screws, hold the screwgun or drill at a right angle to the framing, placing the fastener ⅜" from the panel edge. Space screws evenly along the perimeter and across the field of the panel, following the chart on the opposite page. Do not fasten the entire perimeter and then fasten the field; work along the length or width of the panel, moving across to the sides as you push the drywall tight against the framing. Construction adhesive can be used in addition to screws to create a stronger bond between panel and framing.

Tools & Materials ▸

Work gloves
Eye protection
Screwgun
    or ⅜" drill
Caulk gun

Drywall
Drywall nails
Drywall screws
Construction
    adhesive

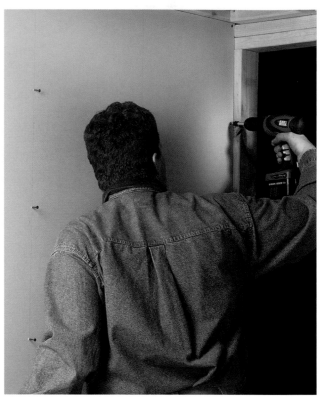

Pre-drive fasteners along the top edge of panels at the location of each framing member to help facilitate installation. Drive fasteners deep enough to hold their place but not enough to penetrate the backside of the panel.

Fastening Drywall ▸

Adhesives create stronger bonds than fasteners and reduce the number of screws needed for panel installation. Apply a ⅜" bead along framing members, stopping 6" from panel edges (left). At butt joints, apply beads to both sides of the joint (right). Panels are then fastened along the perimeter.

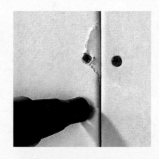

At panel edges, drive fasteners ⅜" from the edges, making sure to hit the framing squarely. If the fastener tears the paper or crumbles the edge, drive another about 2" away from the first.

Recess all screws to provide a space, called a "dimple," for the joint compound. However, driving a screw too far and breaking the paper renders it useless.

Size of Fasteners ▸

Fastener type	Drywall thickness	Minimum fastener length	Fastener type	Drywall thickness	Minimum fastener length
Wood screws (Type W; coarse thread)	3/8" 1/2" 5/8"	1" 1 1/8" 1 1/4"	Steel screws (Type S; fine thread, self-tapping)	3/8" 1/2" 5/8"	3/4" 7/8" 1"

*For multiple layers of drywall, fasteners must penetrate the framing by 7/8". Add the thickness of the two layers plus 7/8" to determine the minimum fastener length.

Maximum Fastener Spacing ▸

Framing	O.C. spacing	Installation style	Maximum screw spacing
Wood joists	16" O.C.	Single panel w/screws	12" O.C.
		Single panel w/adhesive & screws	16" O.C.
		Multiple layers w/screws	
		Base layer:	24" O.C.
		Face layer:	12" O.C.
		Multiple layers w/adhesive & screws:	
		Base layer:	12" O.C.
		Face layer:	12" O.C. (perimeter) 16" O.C. (field)
	24" O.C.	Single panel w/screws	12" O.C.
		Single panel w/adhesive & screws	16" O.C.
		Multiple layers w/screws	12" O.C.
		Multiple layers w/adhesive & screws:	
		Base layer:	12" O.C.
		Face layer:	12" O.C. (perimeter) 16" O.C. (field)
Wood studs	16" O.C.	Single panel w/screws	16" O.C.
		Single panel w/adhesive & screws:	
		Load-bearing partitions	24" O.C.
		Nonload-bearing partitions	24" O.C.
		Multiple layers w/screws	
		Base layer:	24" O.C.
		Face layer:	16" O.C.
		Multiple layers w/adhesive & screws:	
		Base layer:	16" O.C.
		Face layer:	16" O.C. (at top & bottom only)
	24" O.C.	Single panel w/screws	12" O.C.
		Single panel w/adhesive & screws:	
		Load-bearing partitions	16" O.C.
		Nonload-bearing partitions	24" O.C.
		Multiple layers w/screws	
		Base layer:	24" O.C.
		Face layer:	12" O.C.

Framing	O.C. spacing	Installation style	Maximum screw spacing
Wood studs (cont.)	24" O.C.	Multiple layers w/adhesive & screws:	
		Base layer:	12" O.C.
		Face layer:	16" O.C. (at top & bottom only)
Steel studs	16" O.C.	Single panel w/screws	16" O.C.
		Multiple layers w/screws:	
		Base layer	
		Parallel panels	24" O.C.
		Perpendicular	*(see below)
		Face layer:	16" O.C.
		Multiple layers w/adhesive & screws:	
		Base layer:	24" O.C.
		Face layer:	12" O.C. (perimeter) 16" O.C. (field)
Steel studs & resilient channel walls	24" O.C.	Single panel w/screws	12" O.C.
		Multiple layers w/screws:	
		Base layer:	
		Parallel panels	24" O.C.
		Perpendicular	*(see below)
		Face layer:	12" O.C.
		Multiple layers w/adhesive & screws:	
		Base layer:	24" O.C.
		Face layer:	12" O.C. (perimeter) 16" O.C. (field)
Resilient channel ceilings	24" O.C.	Single panel w/screws	12" O.C.
		Multiple layers w/screws:	
		Base layer:	
		Parallel panels	24" O.C.
		Perpendicular	*(see below)
		Face layer:	12" O.C.
		Multiple layers w/adhesive & screws:	
		Base layer:	24" O.C.
		Face layer:	12" O.C. (perimeter) 16" O.C. (field)

*1 screw at each end and 1 screw centered in the field, at each fastener location.
Note: The above information is subject to manufacturer installation specifications.

Hanging Drywall

Hanging drywall is a project that can be completed quickly and easily with a little preplanning and a helping hand.

If you're installing drywall on both the ceilings and the walls, do the ceilings first so the wall panels add extra support for the ceiling panels. When it comes time to install the walls, hang all full panels first, then measure and cut the remaining pieces about ⅛" too small to allow for easy fit.

In nearly every installation, you'll deal with corners. For standard 90° corners, panels most often can butt against one another. But other corners, such as those lacking adequate nailing surfaces or ones that are prone to cracking, may require the use of drywall clips or specialty beads.

Drywall is heavy. While it's possible to hang drywall by yourself, work with a helper whenever possible. A panel lift is also a time and back saver, simplifying installation to ceilings and the upper portion of walls. If you don't want to rent a panel lift, you can make a pair of T-braces, called "deadmen" (see page 29) to hold ceiling panels tight against framing for fastening.

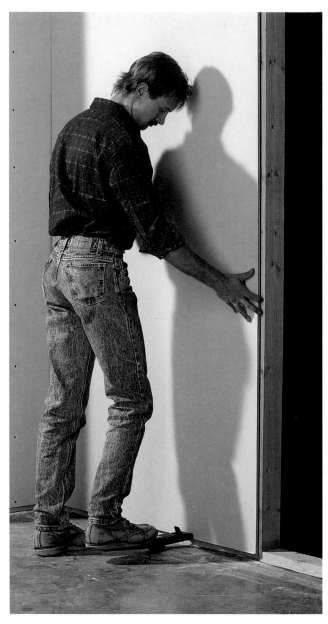

Use a panel lifter to position drywall for fastening. Slide the front end of the lifter beneath the panel edge, then rock backward with your foot to raise the panel into place.

Tip ▶

Where untapered panel ends will be butted together, bevel-cut the outside edges of each panel at 45°, removing about ⅛" of material. This helps prevent the paper from creating a ridge along the seam. Peel off any loose paper from the edge.

Tools & Materials ▶

Work gloves	Drywall screws
Eye protection	Deadmen
T-square	Ladders
Utility knife	Metal flashing
Screwgun or drill	Self-tapping
Panel lift	steel screws
Chalk line	Drywall clips
Drywall panels	

How to Install Drywall on Flat Ceilings

1

Snap a chalk line perpendicular to the joists, 48⅛" from the starting wall.

2

Measure to make sure the first panel will break on the center of a joist. If necessary, cut the panel on the end that abuts the side wall so the panel breaks on the next farthest joist. Load the panel onto a rented panel lift, or use a helper, and lift the panel flat against the joists.

3

Position the panel with the leading edge on the chalk line and the end centered on a joist. Fasten the panel with appropriately sized screws following the fastener spacing chart on page 47.

4

After the first row of panels is installed, begin the next row with a half-panel. This ensures that the butted end joints will be staggered between rows.

How to Install Ceiling Panels Using Deadmen

Construct two 2 × 4 deadmen (see page 29). Lean one against the wall where the panel will be installed, with the top arm a couple inches below the joists. Have a helper assist in lifting the panel and placing the lead edge on the arm. Angle the deadman to pin the panel flush against the joists, but don't use so much pressure you risk damage to the panel.

As the helper supports the panel, use the other deadman to hoist the panel against the joists 24" from the back end. Place ladders at each deadman location and adjust the panel's position by loosening the braces with one hand and moving the panel with the other. Replace the braces and fasten the panel to the framing, following the fastener spacing chart on page 47.

Setting Your Clutch ▸

Professional drywallers drive hundreds, even thousands, of screws per day. Consequently, they invest in pro-quality screwdriving equipment, often with self-feeding coils of screws for rapid-fire work. For DIYers, this equipment can be rented—and may be worth the investment for a very large project. But in most cases a decent quality cordless drill/driver will do nicely. If the drill/driver has a clutch (and most do these days), so much the better. Essentially, a clutch stops the drill's chuck from spinning when the screw encounters a specific amount of resistance. This prevents overdriving of the screw, which is especially important when drywalling (you want to avoid driving the screw far enough into the drywall to break the surface paper). But for the clutch to work properly you need to make sure it is set to the appropriate level of sensitivity. A drill/driver normally has several settings indicated on a shroud or ring near the drill chuck. The highest setting is used for drilling. Basically, the clutch won't disengage the chuck unless it encounters so much resistance that the drill could be damaged. On the lowest setting, the drill will disengage when it encounters only very slight resistance,

as when completing driving a screw into drywall. Before you start driving any drywall screws, test your clutch setting by driving a screw into a piece of scrap drywall and a 2 × 4. Re-set the clutch as needed until it stops driving the moment the screwhead becomes countersunk, creating a very slight dimple. Having the clutch set correctly ensures that your fasteners will have maximum holding power with just enough of a surrounding dimple to give the joint compound a place to go.

Installing Floating Ceiling Joints

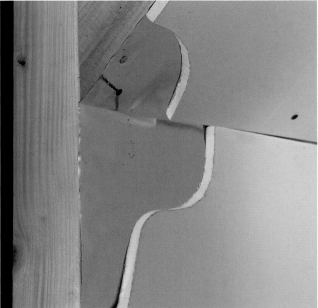

Use metal flashing to prevent cracks along the peak of pitched and cathedral ceilings (left) and the angle between pitched ceilings and sidewalls (right). For both applications, cut metal flashing 16"-wide and to the length of the joint, then bend it lengthwise to match the angle of the peak or corner. Fasten flashing to the framing on one side only, then fasten the panels on that side to the framing. However, fasten the panels at the unfastened side to the flashing only, using self-tapping steel screws. Drive the first row of screws into the framing not less than 12" from the "floating" edge of the panels. *Note: Flexible vinyl bead can also be used for corners prone to cracking.*

Bending Flashing ▸

To bend flashing, make a bending jig by driving screws into a piece of wood, creating a space one-half the width of the flashing when measured from the edge of the board. Clamp the bending jig to a work surface. Lay a piece of flashing flat on the board and bend it over the edge.

For a ceiling with trusses, use drywall clips to eliminate cracks caused by "truss uplift," the seasonal shifting caused by weather changes. Slip clips on the edge of the panel prior to installation, then fasten the clips to the top plate. Fasten the panel to the trusses not less than 18" from the edge of the panel.

How to Install Drywall on Wood-framed Walls

Measure from the wall end or corner to make sure the first panel will break on the center of the stud. If necessary, trim the sheet on the side or end that will be placed in the corner. Mark the stud centers on the panel face and pre-drive screws at each location along the top edge to facilitate fastening. Apply adhesive to the studs, if necessary (see page 46).

With a helper or a drywall lifter, hoist the first panel tight against the ceiling, making sure the side edge is centered on a stud. Push the panel flat against the framing and drive the starter screws to secure the panel. Make any cutouts, then fasten the field of the panel, following the screw spacing on page 47.

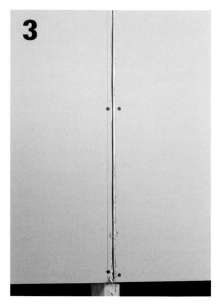

Measure, cut and install the remaining panels along the upper wall. Bevel panel ends slightly, leaving a ⅛" gap between them at the joint. Butt joints can also be installed using back blocking to create a recess (see page 57).

Measure, cut and install the bottom row, butting the panels tight to the upper row and leaving a ½" gap at the floor. Secure to the framing along the top edge using the starter screws, then make all cutouts before fastening the rest of the panel.

Variation: When installing drywall vertically, cut each panel so it's ½" shorter than the ceiling height to allow for expansion. (The gap will be covered by base molding.) Avoid placing tapered edges at outside corners, which makes them difficult to finish.

Installing Drywall at Inside Corners

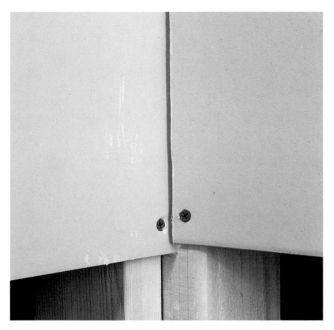

Standard 90° inside corners are installed with the first panel butted against the framing and the adjacent panel butted against the first. The screw spacing remains the same as on a flat wall (see page 47). If the corner is out of plumb or the adjacent wall has an irregular surface, see page 45 for cutting instructions.

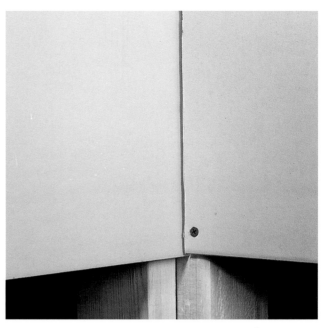

Use a "floating corner" to reduce the chances of popped fasteners and cracks. Install the first panel, fastening only to within one stud bay of the corner. Push the leading edge of the adjacent panel against the first to support the unfastened edge. Fasten the second panel normally, including the corner.

Drywall clips can be used at corners that lack an adequate nailing surface, allowing two panels to be secured to the same stud. Slide clips onto the leading edge of the first panel, with the metal nailing flange outward. Install the panel, fastening the flange to the stud on the adjacent wall with drywall screws. Install the adjacent panel normally.

For off-angle corners, do not overlap panel ends. Install so the panel ends meet at the corner with a ⅛" gap between them.

Installing Drywall at Outside Corners

At outside corners, run panels long so they extend past the corner framing. Fasten the panel in place, then score the backside and snap cut to remove the waste piece.

For standard 90° outside corners, install the first panel so the outside edge is flush with the framing, then install the adjacent panel so it overlaps the end of the first panel.

For off-angle corners or corners where bullnose bead will be installed, do not overlap panel ends. Install each panel so it's leading edge breaks ⅛" from the outside edge of the framing. *Note: Bullnose beads with a slight radius may require a larger reveal.*

For drywall that abuts a finished edge, such as paneling or wood trim, install panels ⅛" from the finished surface, then install a an L-bead to cover the exposed edge (see page 67).

How to Install Drywall Abutting a Finished Surface

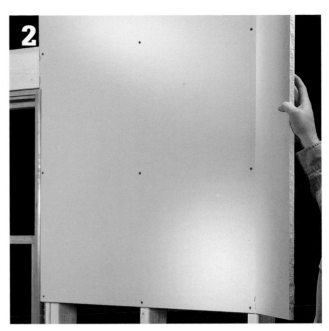

Cut the J-bead (see page 23) to size, then position it flush against the finished surface. Fasten it to the adjacent framing with drywall screws. *Note: Make sure to install J-bead that matches the thickness of your drywall.*

Cut a piece of drywall to size, but let the end run long for final trimming. Slide the end of the drywall into the J-bead until it fits snugly, then fasten the panel to the framing. Score the backside flush with the face of the wall, then snap cut to remove the waste.

Installing Drywall On Gable Walls

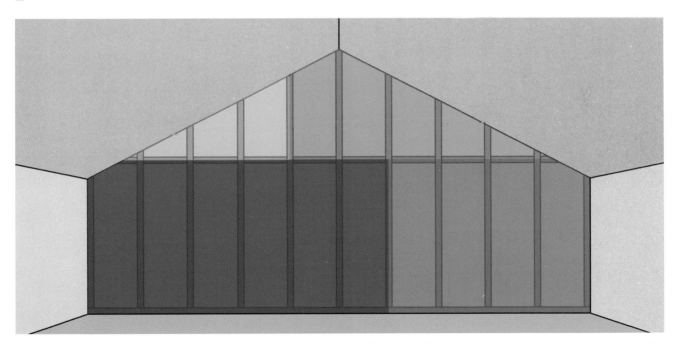

Gables and cathedral ceilings present unique challenges when installing drywall. A few pointers that will help you be successful include: use as many of the panel's factory edges as possible; test-fit each piece directly on the wall; do not force pieces into place, but trim edges as needed instead; install pieces horizontally, with 2 × 4 blocking between the framing member; align horizontal seams, but not vertical seams—stagger these to minimize any twisting in the framing members.

How to Install Drywall on Metal Stud Walls

Metal stud walls in residential construction are generally created with C-shaped 20- to 25-gauge steel studs that are secured at the top and bottom with flanged tracks. If the wall is built correctly, all of the open sides of the C-shaped studs will face in the same direction. Before you begin installing drywall, note which direction the open sides are on.

Begin installing drywall panels in the corner of the room that's closer to the open sides of the metal studs. The first panel should fall midway across a stud, coming from the direction of the open side. Attaching the panel this way will stabilize it; if you install the panel so the free end of the stud flange is loose, it may flex when you attach the drywall screws.

Screw the first panel at each corner using Type S drywall screws (1" is recommended for ½" drywall). These screws have a fairly sharp point that can penetrate the light-gauge metal flanges of the steel studs. As when attaching drywall to wood framing, take care not to overdrive the screws—they tend to take off rather aggressively once they engage in the metal.

Install the second drywall panel, leaving a slight gap at the joint. The new panel should be crossing the closed side of the C-shaped stud. Continue working in this direction until the wall is covered. Taping and seaming are done the same way as for wood framing.

Installing Back Blockers

No matter how good a job you do installing and finishing a butt joint, there's always a chance it'll be visible, even after a coat of paint or layer of wallcovering. Drywall panels can expand and contract as the temperature and humidity in your home changes, causing butted panel ends to push outward and create ridges. While ridging eventually stops (up to a year after installation), you can install back blocking to help prevent the problem before it even starts.

Back blocking creates a recessed butt joint by slightly bending panel ends into the bay between framing members, where they are secured to a floating blocking device with drywall screws. The result is a recessed joint that approximates a tapered joint and can be finished just as easily using standard techniques. And because the joint floats between framing members, it's unlikely to crack or ridge. Back blocking can be used for both walls and ceilings.

Although commercial back blockers are available, you can easily make your own back blocker by attaching narrow strips of ¼" hardboard to the edges of a 6 to 10" wide strip of ¾" plywood. When placed behind a drywall butt joint, the hardboard strips will create a thin space, into which the edges of the drywall will be deflected when it's screwed to the back blocker. The instructions below show a homemade back blocker in use.

Tools & Materials ▸

Work gloves	Drywall screws
Eye protection	¾ × 10 × 48"
Screwgun	plywood
or ⅜" drill	¼ × ¾ × 48"
Tape measure	hardboard

How to Install a Back Blocker

Hang the first drywall panel so the end breaks midway between the framing members. Position the back blocker behind the panel so the end covers half of the wood center strip, then fasten every 6" along the end.

Install the second panel so it butts against the first panel. Fasten the end of the second panel to the back blocker with drywall screws every 6". The screws will pull the end of the panel into the blocker, creating the recessed joint.

Hanging Cementboard

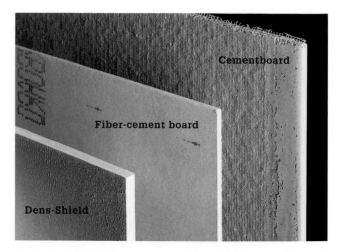

Use tile backer board as the substrate for tile walls in wet areas. Unlike drywall, tile backer won't break down and cause damage if water gets behind the tile. The three basic types of tile backer are cementboard, fiber-cement board, and Dens-Shield.

Though water cannot damage either cementboard or fiber-cement board, it can pass through them. To protect the framing members, install a water barrier of 4-mil plastic or 15# building paper behind the backer.

Dens-Shield has a waterproof acrylic facing that provides the water barrier. It cuts and installs much like drywall, but requires galvanized screws to prevent corrosion and must be sealed with caulk at all untaped joints and penetrations.

Common tile backers are cementboard, fiber-cement board, and Dens-Shield. Cementboard is made from portland cement and sand reinforced by an outer layer of fiberglass mesh. Fiber-cement board is made similarly, but with a fiber reinforcement integrated throughout the panel. Dens-Shield is a water-resistant gypsum board with a waterproof acrylic facing.

Tools & Materials ▸

Work gloves	Small masonry bits	Stapler	Latex-portland
Eye protection	Hammer	4-mil plastic sheeting	cement mortar
Utility knife or carbide-	Jigsaw with a carbide	Cementboard	15# building paper
tipped cutter	grit blade	1¼" cementboard screws	Spacers
T-square	Taping knives	Cementboard joint tape	Screwgun

How to Hang Cementboard

Staple a water barrier of 4-mil plastic sheeting or 15# building paper over the framing. Overlap seams by several inches, and leave the sheets long at the perimeter. *Note: Framing for cementboard must be 16" on-center; steel studs must be 20-gauge.*

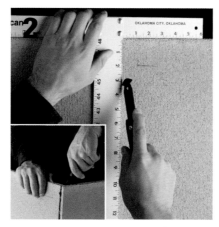

Cut cementboard by scoring through the mesh just below the surface with a utility knife or carbide-tipped cutter. Snap the panel back, then cut through the back-side mesh (inset). *Note: For tile applications, the rough face of the board is the front.*

Make cutouts for pipes and other penetrations by drilling a series of holes through the board, using a small masonry bit. Tap the hole out with a hammer or a scrap of pipe. Cut holes along edges with a jigsaw and carbide grit blade.

Install the sheets horizontally. Where possible, use full pieces to avoid butted seams, which are difficult to fasten. If there are vertical seams, stagger them between rows. Leave a ⅛" gap between sheets at vertical seams and corners. Use spacers to set the bottom row of panels ¼" above the tub or shower base. Fasten the sheets with 1¼" cementboard screws, driven every 8" for walls and every 6" for ceilings. Drive the screws at least ½" from the edges to prevent crumbling. If the studs are steel, don't fasten within 1" of the top track.

Cover the joints and corners with cementboard joint tape (alkali-resistant fiberglass mesh) and latex-portland cement mortar (thin-set). Apply a layer of mortar with a taping knife, embed the tape into the mortar, then smooth and level the mortar.

Finishing Cementboard

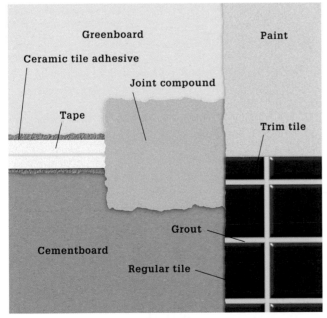

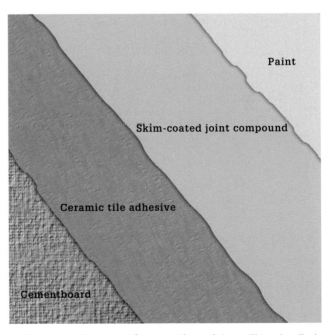

To finish a joint between cementboard and greenboard, seal the joint and exposed cementboard with ceramic tile adhesive, a mixture of four parts adhesive to one part water. Embed paper joint tape into the adhesive, smoothing the tape with a taping knife. Allow the adhesive to dry, then finish the joint with at least two coats of all-purpose drywall joint compound.

To finish small areas of cementboard that will not be tiled, seal the cementboard with ceramic tile adhesive, a mixture of four parts adhesive to one part water, then apply a skim-coat of all-purpose drywall joint compound using a 12" drywall knife. Then prime and paint the wall.

Finishing Drywall

The process of finishing drywall involves distinct steps: tape seams; cover fastener heads; install corner bead; apply a second coat of joint compound; apply a third coat of joint compound; sand (if necessary); apply a skim coat or finished texture (optional); prime and paint.

The process is not as complicated or time-consuming as the list of tasks may make it sound. By simply doing careful work when applying finishing materials you can eliminate most of the sanding (which happens to be the messiest part). The most important part of the job—and the area where most people take ill-advised shortcuts —is in the three rounds of joint compound application. The key here is to use taping knives of increasingly larger size, ending with a knife that has a blade at least 12" wide. By feathering out the joint compound on each side of the seam with a 12" knife, you will create a smooth compound layer that's a full 24" wide and virtually impossible to detect after the wall is primed and painted.

Once the wall is mudded, a light sanding and a coat of drywall primer are all that's needed to prepare for a fine painted finish. If you wish, you can apply a texture or a skim coat to the wall or ceiling before painting to create an interesting surface.

In this chapter:

- Recommended Levels of Drywall Finish
- Installing Corner Bead
- Taping Drywall Seams
- Fixing Problems & Final Inspection
- Sanding Drywall
- Textures & Skim Coats
- Priming & Painting Drywall

Recommended Levels of Drywall Finish

The main purpose of finishing drywall is to create an acceptable base surface for the desired decorative finish. For example, walls and ceilings that will be illuminated by bright light or finished with gloss paint or thin wallcovering require a smooth, consistent surface to prevent taped seams, covered fasteners and minor imperfections from showing through—a condition called *photographing*. On the other hand, surfaces that will be sprayed with a texture don't need as polished a drywall finish, and areas that only need to meet fire codes may be acceptable with a single tape coat.

For years, there were no universal guidelines for what was considered an "acceptable" drywall finish, which often left contractors and homeowners at odds over what "industry standard finish" actually meant. But recently four major trade associations devised a set of guidelines that have been accepted industry-wide. Below are their recommendations for finishing drywall, as found in document GA-214-96, entitled "Recommended Levels of Gypsum Board Finish." Each entry describes the minimum level of finish recommended. The full document can be downloaded from the Gypsum Association's website (gypsum.org/downloads.html).

LEVEL 0

"No taping, finishing, or accessories required."

This level of finish may be useful in temporary construction or whenever the final decoration has not been determined.

LEVEL 1

"All joints and interior angles shall have tape set in joint compound. Surface shall be free of excess joint compound. Tool marks and ridges are acceptable."

Frequently specified in plenum areas above ceilings, in attics, in areas where the assembly would generally be concealed or in building service corridors, and other areas not normally open to public view. Accessories (beads, trims, or moldings) optional at specifier discretion in corridors and other areas with pedestrian traffic.

Some degree of sound and smoke control is provided; in some geographic areas this level is referred to as "firetaping." Where a fire-resistance rating is required for the gypsum board assembly, details of construction shall be in accordance with reports of fire tests of assemblies that have met the fire-rating requirement. Tape and fastener heads need not be covered with joint compound.

LEVEL 2

"All joints and interior angles shall have tape embedded in joint compound and wiped with a joint knife leaving a thin coating of joint compound over all joints and interior angles. Fastener heads and accessories shall be covered with a coat of joint compound. Surface shall be free of excess joint compound. Tool marks and ridges are acceptable. Joint compound applied over the body of the tape at the time of tape embedment shall be considered a separate coat of joint compound and shall satisfy the conditions of this level."

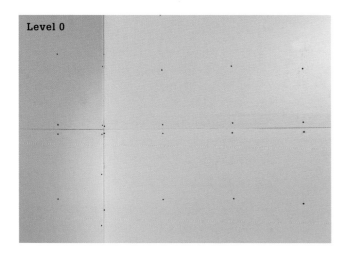

Level 0

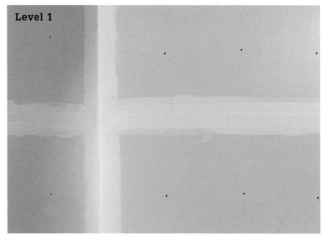

Level 1

Specified where water-resistant gypsum backing board (ASTM C 630) is used as a substrate for tile; may be specified in garages, warehouse storage, or other similar areas where surface appearance is not of primary concern.

LEVEL 3

"All joints and interior angles shall have tape embedded in joint compound and one additional coat of joint compound applied over all joints and interior angles. Fastener heads and accessories shall be covered with two separate coats of joint compound. All joint compound shall be smooth and free of tool marks and ridges. *Note: It is recommended that the prepared surface be coated with a drywall primer prior to the application of final finishes. See painting/wallcovering specification in this regard."*

Typically specified in appearance areas which are to receive heavy- or medium-texture (spray or hand applied) finishes before final painting, or where heavy-grade wallcoverings are to be applied as the final decoration. This level of finish is not recommended where smooth painted surfaces or light to medium wallcoverings are specified.

LEVEL 4

"All joints and interior angles shall have tape embedded in joint compound and two separate coats of joint compound applied over all flat joints and one separate coat of joint compound applied over interior angles. Fastener heads and accessories shall be covered with three separate coats of joint compound. All joint compound shall be smooth and free of tool marks and ridges. *Note: It is recommended that the prepared surface be coated with a drywall primer prior to the application of final finishes. See painting/ wallcovering specification in this regard."*

This level should be specified where flat paints, light textures, or wallcoverings are to be applied. In critical lighting areas, flat paints applied over light textures tend to reduce joint photographing. Gloss, semi-gloss, and enamel paints are not recommended over this level of finish.

The weight, texture, and sheen level of wallcoverings applied over this level of finish should be carefully evaluated. Joints and fasteners must be adequately concealed if the wallcovering material is lightweight, contains limited pattern, has a gloss finish, or any combination of these finishes is present. Unbacked vinyl wallcoverings are not recommended over this level of finish.

LEVEL 5

"All joints and interior angles shall have tape embedded in joint compound and two separate coats of joint compound applied over all flat joints and one separate coat of joint compound applied over interior angles. Fastener heads and accessories shall be covered with three separate coats of joint compound. A thin skim coat of joint compound or a material manufactured especially for this purpose, shall be applied to the entire surface. The surface shall be smooth and free of tool marks and ridges. *Note: It is recommended that the prepared surface be coated with a drywall primer prior to the application of finish paint. See painting specification in this regard."*

This level of finish is highly recommended where gloss, semi-gloss, enamel, or non-textured flat paints are specified or where severe lighting conditions occur. This highest quality finish is the most effective method to provide a uniform surface and minimize the possibility of joint photographing and of fasteners showing through the final decoration.

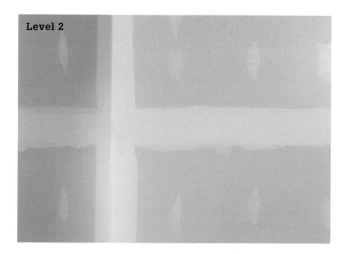

Level 2

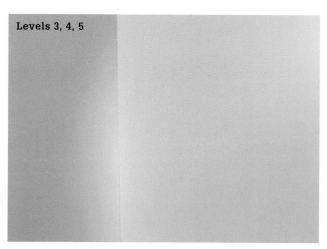

Levels 3, 4, 5

Installing Corner Bead

After the drywall is hung, the next step is to install corner bead to protect outside corners, soffits, drywall-finished openings, and any other outside angles. Corner bead provides a clean, solid-edge wall corner that can withstand moderate abuse. It is available in a variety of styles for a variety of applications (see page 23). The three most common types are metal, vinyl and paper-faced beads.

Metal beads can be fastened with nails, screws, or a crimper tool. Vinyl beads are easily installed with spray adhesive and staples, or can be embedded in compound, similar to paper-faced beads.

A number of specialty beads are also available, including flexible archway beads for curved corners and J-bead for covering panel ends that meet finished surfaces. Decorative bullnose beads and caps for 2- and 3-way corners are easy ways to add interesting detail to a room.

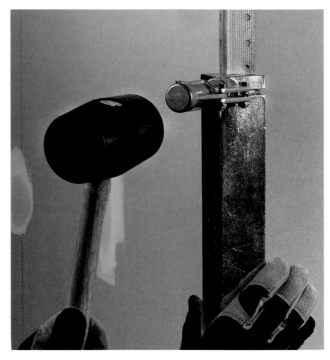

Metal corner bead installed over steel framing can be fastened using a crimper tool. Cut the bead to size and position in the corner (see step 1 below), then crimp every 4 to 6".

Tools & Materials ▸

Work gloves	Stapler	1¼" drywall screws	½" staples
Eye protection	Hammer	1½" ring-shank drywall nails	Archway bead
Aviation snips	Corner bead	Spray adhesive	Metal file
Screwgun or drill			

How to Install Metal Corner Bead

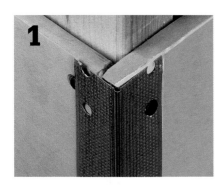

Cut metal corner bead to length using aviation snips, leaving a ½" gap at the floor. Position the bead so the raised spine is centered over the corner and the flanges are flat against both walls.

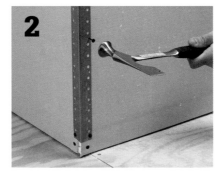

Starting at the top, fasten the bead flanges with drywall nails, driven every 9" and about ¼" from the edge. Alternate sides with each screw to keep the bead centered. The screws must not project beyond the raised spine.

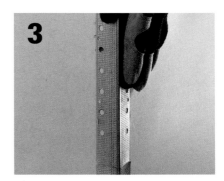

Use full lengths of corner bead where possible. If you must join two lengths, cut the two pieces to size, then butt together the finished ends. Make sure the ends are perfectly aligned and the spine is straight along the length of the corner. File ends, if necessary.

How to Install Vinyl Corner Bead

Cut vinyl bead to length and test fit over corner. Spray vinyl adhesive evenly along the entire length of the corner, then along the bead.

Quickly install the bead, pressing the flanges into the adhesive. Fasten the bead in place with ½" staples every 8".

How to Install Corner Bead at Three-way Corners

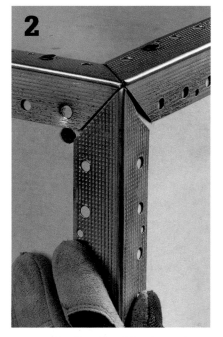

File Edges ▸

Where two or more outside corners meet, trim back the overlapping flanges of each bead to 45° mitered ends using aviation snips. The ends don't have to match perfectly, but they should not overlap.

Fasten the first bead in place, then test fit each subsequent piece, trimming any overlapping flanges. Align the tips of the two pieces and fasten in place. Install additional beads in the same way.

Blunt any sharp edges or points created by metal bead at three-way corners using a metal file.

How to Install Flexible Bead for an Archway

Install standard corner bead on the straight lengths of the corners (see pages 64 to 65) so it is ½" from the floor and 2" from the start of the arch.

Flatten flexible vinyl bead along the archway to determine the length needed, then add 3". Cut two pieces of bead to this length, one for each side of the archway.

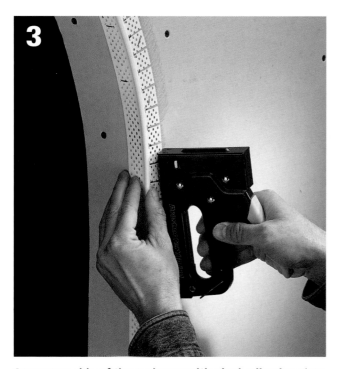

Spray one side of the archway with vinyl adhesive, then spray the bead. Immediately install the bead—work from one end, pushing the bead tight into the corner along the arch. Secure with ½" staples every 2". Trim the overlapping end so it meets the end of the straight length of corner bead.

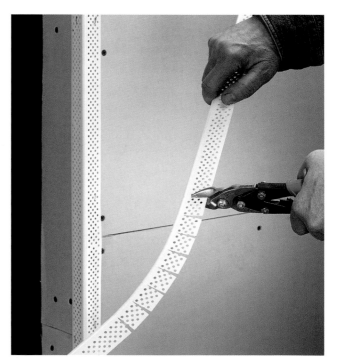

Variation: To substitute for flexible bead, snip one flange of standard vinyl bead at 1" intervals. Be careful not to cut into or through the spine.

How to Install L-Bead

1

L-bead caps the ends of drywall panels that abut finished surfaces such as paneling or wood trim, providing a finished edge. The drywall is installed ⅛" from the finished surface, then the L-bead is positioned tight against the panel, so its finished edge covers the edge of the adjacent surface.

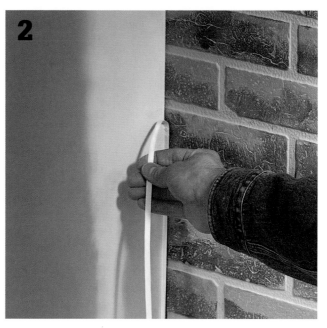

2

Fasten L-bead to the drywall with ½" staples or drywall screws every 6", then finish with a minimum of three coats of compound (see pages 69 to 75). After final sanding, peel back the protective strip to expose the finished edge of the L-bead.

Installing Vinyl Bullnose Corner Bead ▸

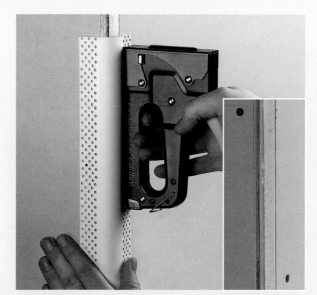

Vinyl bullnose corner bead is installed with vinyl adhesive and ½" staples, just like standard vinyl bead (see page 65). However, bullnose beads that have shallow curves may require that the ends of drywall panels be cut back (inset).

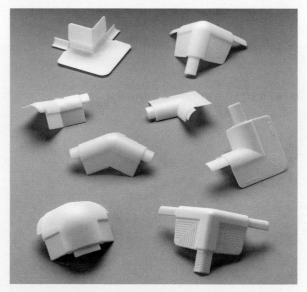

Drywall manufacturers offer a variety of corner caps to ease the process of finishing soffits and other openings trimmed out with bullnose corner bead.

Taping Drywall Seams

Finishing newly installed drywall is satisfying work that requires patience and some basic skill, but it's easier than most people think. Beginners make their biggest, and most lasting, mistakes by rushing the job and applying too much compound in an attempt to eliminate coats. But even for professionals, drywall finishing involves three steps, and sometimes more, plus the final sanding.

The first step is the taping coat, when you tape the seams between the drywall panels. The taping is critical to the success of the entire job, so take your time here, and make sure the tape is smooth and fully adhered before it's allowed to dry. If you're using standard metal corner bead on the outside corners, install it before starting the taping coat; paper-faced beads go on after the tape. The screw heads get covered with compound at the beginning of each coat.

After the taping comes the second, or filler, coat. This is when you leave the most compound on the wall, filling in the majority of each depression. With the filler coat, the walls start to look good, but they don't have to be perfect; the third coat will take care of minor imperfections. Lightly scrape the second coat with a taping knife, then apply the final coat. If you still see imperfections, add more compound before sanding.

For best results, especially with fiberglass tape, use a setting-type compound for the taping coat. It creates a strong bond and shrinks very little. Because setting-type compound hardens by chemical reaction, once it begins to set up the process cannot be slowed or stopped, rendering excess compound unusable. Make sure to prepare only as much as you can use in the amount of work time specified by the manufacturer. Use lightweight setting-type compound because it is easier to sand.

For the other two coats, use an all-purpose compound. These drying-type compounds are available premixed and can be thinned with water if setup begins prematurely. Add small amounts of water to avoid over-thinning and mix using a hand masher. If compound is too thin, add thicker compound from another container. Remix periodically if the liquid begins to separate and rise to the top. If pre-mixed compound is moldy or foul-smelling, it is unusable and must be discarded.

Allow each coat of compound to set up and dry thoroughly before applying the next coat. Setting time is dependent on a number of factors, such as size of project and type of compound used, but for most finishing projects, count on one day per coat—a total

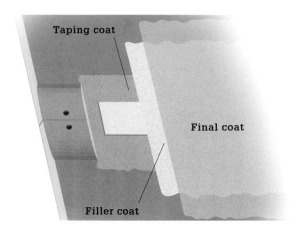

of three days. Refer to the manufacturer's instructions for product specifications. To speed up the process, compound accelerants are available, or use a fan.

Before you begin, make sure all drywall panels are hung correctly, all corner beads are in place, and all damaged areas are repaired. Use a screwdriver to set any protruding screw heads. Finally, make sure the work area is clear of any unnecessary obstacles, tools, and materials.

As you work, keep your compound smooth and workable by mixing it in the mud pan frequently, folding it over with the drywall knife. Try to remove dried chunks, and throw away any mud that gets dirty or has been added to and scraped off the wall too many times. Always let your compound dry completely between coats. If you have a large ceiling area to finish, it may be practical to rent a pair of drywall stilts.

Tools & Materials ▸

Work gloves	Mud pan
Eye protection	Setting-type
Screwdriver	joint compound
Utility knife	(for tape coat)
5-gallon bucket	All-purpose compound
½" electric drill with	(for filler and
mixing paddle	finish coat)
Hand masher	Cool potable water
4", 6", 10", and 12"	Paper joint tape
taping knives	Self-adhesive fiberglass
Inside corner	mesh tape
taping knife	

Preparing Joint Compound

Mix powdered setting-type compound with cool, potable water in a clean 5-gal. bucket, following the manufacturer's directions. All tools and materials must be clean—dirty water, old compound, and other contaminants will affect compound set time and quality.

Use a heavy-duty drill with a mixing paddle to thoroughly mix compound to a stiff, yet workable consistency (see below). Use a low speed to avoid whipping air into the compound. Do not overwork setting-type compound, as it will begin setup. For powdered drying-type compound, remix after fifteen minutes. Clean tools thoroughly immediately after use.

Use a hand masher to loosen premixed compound. If the compound has been around awhile and is stiff, add a little water and mix to an even consistency.

Joint compound should appear smooth in consistency and stiff enough so as not to slide off a trowel or taping knife.

How to Apply the Taping Coat

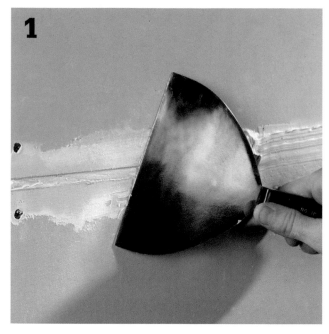

Inspect the entire drywall installation and fill any gaps wider than ¼" with setting-type compound. Smooth off excess so it's flush with the panel face. Also remove any loose paper and fill in with compound.

Using a 4" or 6" taping knife, smear compound over each screw head, forcing it into the depression. Firmly drag the knife in the opposite direction, removing excess compound from the panel surface.

Variation: Cover an entire row of screw heads in the field of a panel with one steady, even pass of compound. Use a 6" taping knife and apply a thin coat.

On tapered seams, apply an even bed layer of setting-type compound over the seam, about ⅛" thick and 6" wide using a 6" taping knife. *Note: With paper tape, you can use premixed taping or all-purpose compound instead.*

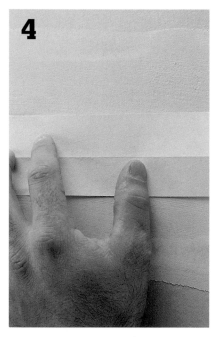

Center the tape over the seam and lightly embed it in the compound, making sure the tape is smooth and straight. At the end of the seam, tear off the tape so it extends all the way into inside corners and up to the corner bead at outside corners.

5

Smooth the tape with the taping knife, working out from the center. Apply enough pressure to force compound from underneath the tape, so the tape is flat and has a thin layer beneath it.

6

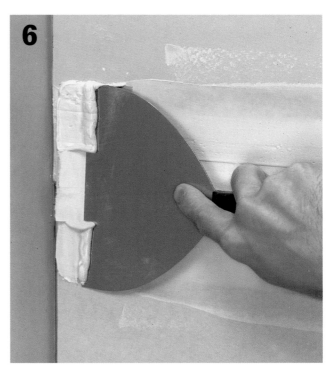

At inside corners, smooth the final bit of tape by reversing the knife and carefully pushing it toward the corner. Carefully remove excess compound along the edges of the bed layer with the taping knife.

7

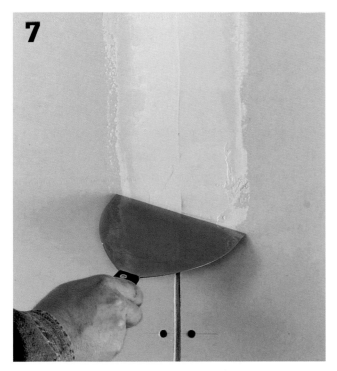

On butt seams, apply an even ⅛"-thick, 4"-wide bed layer of setting-type compound using a 4" taping knife. Work in one direction and completely fill the V-notch.

8

Center the tape over the butt seam and lightly embed it in the compound. As you smooth the tape, apply enough pressure to leave only a ¹⁄₁₆" layer of compound beneath the tape. Smooth the edges to remove excess compound. Allow to dry and then coat with a thin layer of compound.

(continued)

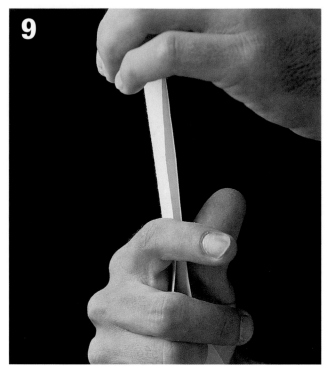

9

Tape inside corners by folding precreased paper tape in half to create a 90° angle.

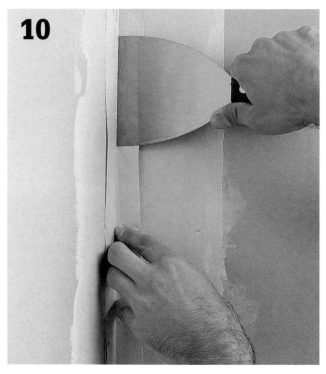

10

Apply an even layer of compound, about ⅛" thick and 3" wide, to both sides of the corner using a 4" taping knife. Embed the tape into the compound using a taping knife.

11

Carefully smooth and flatten both sides of the tape, removing excess compound to leave only a thin layer beneath. Make sure the center of the tape is aligned straight with the corner.

Tool Tip ▶

An inside corner knife can embed both sides of the tape in one pass—draw the knife along the tape, applying enough pressure to leave a thin layer of compound beneath. Feather each side using a straight 6" taping knife, if necessary.

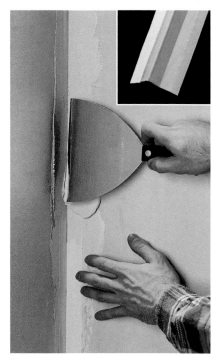

Variation: Paper-faced metal inside corner bead produces straight, durable corners with little fuss. To install the bead, embed it into a thin layer of compound, then smooth the paper, as with a paper-tape inside corner.

12

Finish outside corner bead with a 6" knife. Apply the compound while dragging the knife along the raised spine of the bead. Make a second pass to feather the outside edge of the compound, then a third dragging along the bead again. Smooth any areas where the corner bead meets taped corners or seams.

Variation: To install paper-faced outside corner bead, spread an even layer of compound on each side of the corner using a 6" taping knife. Press the bead into the compound and smooth the paper flanges with the knife.

How to Apply Mesh Tape

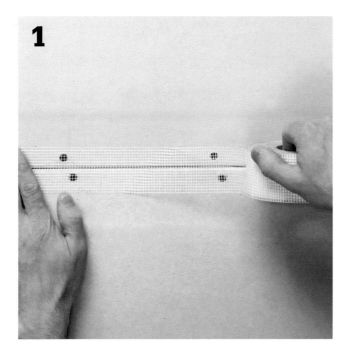

1

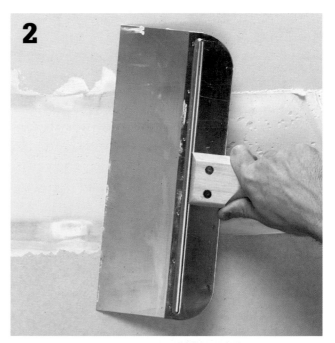

2

To use self-adhesive mesh tape on seams, apply the tape over the seam center so it's straight and flat. Run mesh tape to corners, then cut using a sharp utility knife.

Coat the mesh with an even layer of compound, about ⅛" thick using a 6" taping knife. Smooth the joint with a 10" or 12" knife, removing excess compound. *Note: Use setting-type compound for the first coat.*

How to Apply the Filler Coat

After the taping coat has dried completely, scrape off any ridges and chunks. Begin second-coating at the screw heads using a 6" taping knife and all-purpose compound (see page 70). *Note: Setting-type compound and drying-type topping compound are also acceptable.*

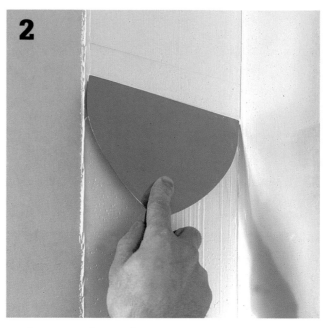

Apply an even layer of compound to both sides of each inside corner using a 6" taping knife. Smooth one side at a time, holding the blade about 15° from horizontal and lightly dragging the point along the corner. Make a second pass to remove excess compound along the outer edges. Repeat, if necessary.

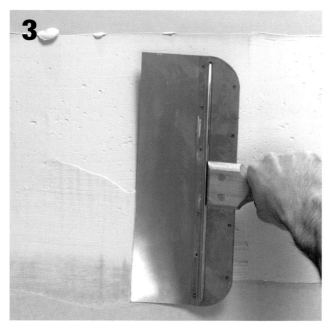

Coat tapered seams with an even layer of compound using a 12" taping knife. Whenever possible, apply the coat in one direction and smooth it in the opposite. Feather the sides of the compound first, holding the blade almost flat and applying pressure to the outside of the blade, so the blade just skims over the center of the seam.

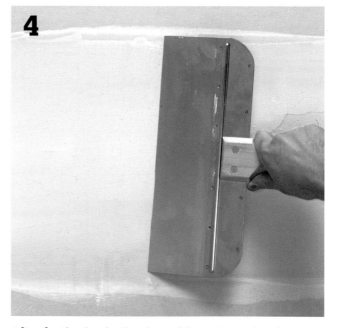

After feathering both edges of the compound, make a pass down the center of the seam, applying even pressure to the blade. This pass should leave the seam smooth and even, with the edges feathered out to nothing. The joint tape should be completely covered.

5

For butt seams, use the same technique as for tapered seams, however, feather the edges out 8 to 10" on each side to help mask the seam. Apply compound in thin layers and smooth out as needed.

6

Second-coat the outside corners, one side at a time using a 12" knife. Apply an even layer of compound, then feather the outside edge by applying pressure to the outside of the knife—enough so that the blade flexes and removes most of the compound along the edge but leaves the corner intact. Make a second pass with the blade riding along the raised spine, applying even pressure.

How to Apply the Final Coat

1

After the filler coat has dried, lightly scrape all of the joints, then third-coat the screws. Apply the final coat, following the same steps used for the filler coat—but do the seams first, then the outside corners, followed by the inside corners. Use a 12" knife and spread the compound a few inches wider than the joints in the filler coat. Remove most of the wet compound, filling scratches and low spots but leaving only traces elsewhere. Make several passes, if necessary, until the surface is smooth and there are no knife tracks or other imperfections. Carefully blend intersecting joints so there's no visible transition.

How to Flat-tape

Trim any loose paper along the drywall edge with a utility knife. If the gap between the drywall and the object is wider than ¼", fill it with joint compound and let it dry. Cover the joint with self-adhesive mesh joint tape, butting the tape's edge against the object without overlapping the object.

Cover the tape with a 4"-wide layer of setting-type taping compound. Smooth the joint, leaving just enough compound to conceal the tape. Let the first coat dry completely, then add two more thin coats using a 6" taping knife. Feather the outside edge of the joint to nothing.

How to Round Inside Corners

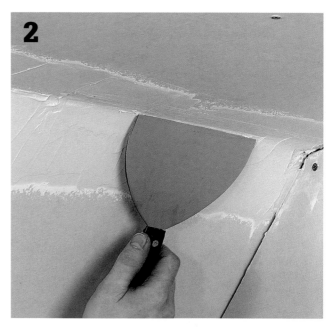

To soften off-angle inside corners, round them off. Center self-adhesive fiberglass mesh tape over the seam, and smooth it flat. Apply a ⅛" thick layer of compound 4" wide along each side of the mesh using a 6" taping knife. *Note: Use setting-type compound to prevent significant shrinkage.*

Lightly drag the knife across the seam, perpendicular to the corner, to sculpt a rounded base for the filler coat. Work in the same direction along the entire length of the seam, then make a second pass, pulling the knife across in the opposite direction.

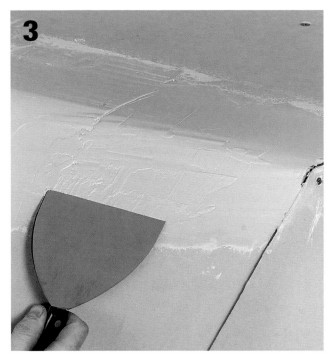

3

Once the tape is completely covered, smooth out any ridges and feather the edges of the compound along the length of the seam.

4

After the tape coat is dry, apply another ⅛" layer of setting-type compound along the seam, then use a 12" taping knife to create the rounded corner, following the same technique as in step 2.

5

After the fill coat has dried, lightly scrape ridges and high spots, then apply a thin layer of all-purpose or topping compound for the final coat, following the same technique as for the previous two coats.

Variation: Flexible corner beads are available for off-angle joints that are prone to cracking, such as those between pitched ceilings and flat kneewalls. The vinyl center crease flexes along with normal structural shifts. Install flexible bead with adhesive or embed it in compound; keep the center crease free of compound.

Fixing Problems & Final Inspection

After the final coat of joint compound has dried but before you begin sanding, inspect the entire finish job for flaws. If you discover scrapes, pitting or other imperfections, add another coat of joint compound. Repair any damaged or overlooked areas such as cracked seams and over-cut holes for electrical boxes prior to sanding.

During your inspection, make sure to check that all seams are acceptably feathered out. To check seams, hold a level or 12" taping knife perpendicularly across the seam; fill concave areas with extra layers of compound and correct any convex seams that crown more than ⅟₁₆".

Tools & Materials ▸

Work gloves
Eye protection
6" and 12"
   taping knives
Sanding block
   or pole sander
All-purpose joint
   compound

Utility knife
Self-adhesive
   fiberglass
   mesh tape
220-grit sanding
   screen or
   150-grit sandpaper

Scratches, dents, and other minor imperfections can be smoothed over with a thin coat of all-purpose compound.

Common Taping Problems

Pitting occurs when compound is overmixed or applied with too little pressure to force out trapped air bubbles. Pitting can be fixed with a thin coat of compound. If trapped air bubbles are present, scrape lightly before covering with compound.

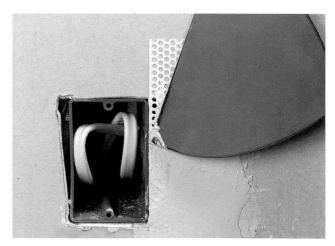

Mis-cut holes for electrical boxes can be flat taped. Cover the gap with self-adhesive mesh tape and cover with three coats of all-purpose compound. Precut repair patches are also available (shown).

Concave seams can be filled with an extra layer or two of all-purpose compound, repeating the filler and final coats (see pages 74 to 75).

For seams crowned more than $\frac{1}{16}$", carefully sand along the center (see pages 81 to 83), but do not expose the tape. Check the seam with a level. If it's still crowned, add a layer of compound with a 12" knife, removing all of it along the seam's center and feathering it out toward the outside edges. After it dries, apply a final coat, if necessary.

Bubbled or loose tape occurs when the bed layer is too thin, which causes a faulty bond between the tape and compound. Cut out small, soft areas with a utility knife and retape. Large runs of loose tape will have to be fully removed before retaping.

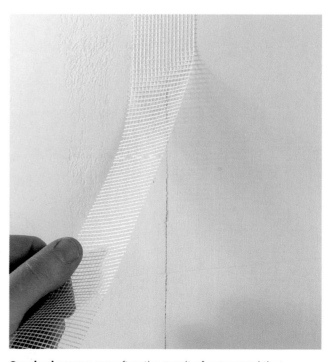

Cracked seams are often the result of compound that has dried too quickly or shrunk. Re-tape the seam if the existing tape and compound is intact; otherwise, cut out any loose material. In either case, make sure to fill the crack with compound.

Sanding Drywall

Sanding is the final step in finishing drywall. The goal is to remove excess joint compound and crowned seams, smooth out tool and lap marks and feather the edges so they blend into the panel surface. How much sanding is required depends on the quality of the taping job and the level of finish you need for the final decoration (see pages 62 to 63).

Sanding drywall is a two-step process: pole sanding to remove excess compound and feather edges, and hand sanding to take care of the final smoothing work.

Pole sanders have a flat head on a swivel that holds sandpaper or sanding screen. The length of the pole keeps you distanced from dust and brings ceiling seams within reach. You don't have to apply much pressure to get results—simply push the head along the seam and let the weight of the tool do the work. You can use a 120-grit sanding screen or sandpaper for joints finished with all-purpose compound, or you can use 150-grit on lightweight or topping compounds, which are softer.

Hand sanding can be done with a block sander or dry sanding sponge. The object of this step is to smooth all the joints and create a uniform surface, so again you need not apply much pressure to get the job done. Use 150- to 220-grit sanding screen or sandpaper for final sanding.

As you work, make sure to sand only the compound rather than the panels. Face paper can scuff easily, necessitating a thin coat of compound to repair. Do not use power sanders on drywall; they are too difficult to control. Even brief lingering can remove too much compound or mar panels.

Sanding drywall is a messy job. The fine dust generated will easily find its way into all areas of the home if the work area is not contained. Sealing all doorways and cracks with sheet plastic and masking tape will help prevent dust from leaving the work zone. However, wet sanding may be more practical in some instances. With wet sanding, or sponging, the abrasive papers and screens are replaced by a damp sponge that is used to smooth the water-soluble compound and blend it with the surface. Very little dust becomes airborne.

But if your goal is to eradicate dust, your best bet is to use a dust-free sanding system. Available at most rental centers, dust-free systems contain hoses with sanding attachments that connect to a wet/dry vacuum to cut dust by nearly ninety-five percent. A water filter can be added to the system to capture most of the dust and spare your vacuum's filter.

Tools & Materials ▸

Work gloves	Broom or towel
Eye protection	N95-rated dust mask
Swivel-joint	Eye goggles
pole sander	Sheet plastic
Hand-sander block	2" painter's tape
Work light	120-, 150- and
Dry sanding sponge	220-grit
Wet sanding sponge	sandpaper or
Wet/dry	sanding screens
shop vacuum	6" taping knife

Mark Low Spots ▸

As you work, if you oversand or discover low spots that require another coat of compound, mark the area with a piece of painter's tape for repair after you finish sanding. Make sure to wipe away dust so the tape sticks to the surface.

Minimizing Dust

Use sheet plastic and 2" masking tape to help confine dust to the work area. Cover all doorways, cabinets, built-ins, and any gaps or other openings with plastic, sealing all four edges with tape—the fine dust produced by sanding can find its way through the smallest cracks.

Prop a fan in an open window so it blows outside to help pull dust out of the work area during sanding. Open only one window in the space to prevent a cross-breeze.

How to Sand Drywall

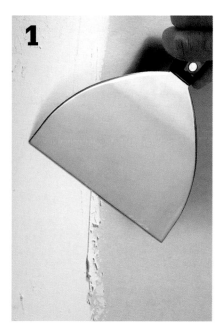

1

2

Prior to sanding, knock down any ridges, chunks or tool marks using a 6" taping knife. Do not apply too much pressure—you don't want to dig into the compound, only remove the excess.

Lightly sand all seams and outside corners using a pole sander with 220-grit sanding screen or 150-grit sandpaper. Work in the direction of the joints, applying even pressure to smooth transitions and high areas. Don't sand out depressions; fill them with compound and resand. Be careful not to over-sand or expose joint tape.

3

Inside corners often are finished with only one or two thin coats of compound over the tape. Sand the inside edge of joints only lightly and smooth the outside edge carefully; inside corners will be sanded by hand later.

4

Fine-sand the seams, outside corners, and fastener heads using a sanding block with 150- to 220-grit sanding screen or sandpaper. As you work, use your hand to feel for defects along the compound. A bright work light angled to highlight seams can help reveal problem areas.

5

To avoid damage from over-sanding, use a 150-grit dry sanding sponge to sand inside corners. The sides of sanding sponges also contain grit, allowing you to sand both sides of a corner at once to help prevent over-sanding.

6

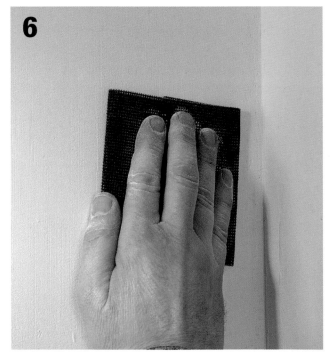

For tight or hard-to-reach corners, fold a piece of sanding screen or sandpaper in thirds and sand the area carefully. Rather than using just your fingertips, try to flatten your hand as much as possible to spread out the pressure to avoid sanding too deep.

7

Repair depressions, scratches or exposed tape due to over-sanding after final sanding is complete. Wipe the area with a dry cloth to remove dust, then apply a thin coat of all-purpose compound. Allow to dry thoroughly, then resand.

8

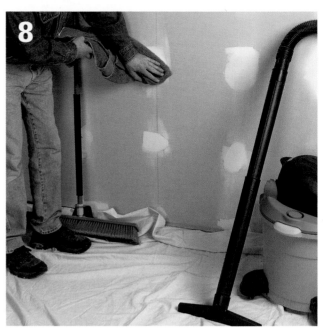

With sanding complete, remove dust from the panels with a dry towel or soft broom. Use a wet-dry vacuum to clean out all electrical boxes and around floors, windows and doors, then carefully roll up sheet plastic and discard. Finally, damp mop the floor to remove any remaining dust.

Dust-free Drywall Sanding

Wet sanding is a dust-free alternative to dry sanding. Use a high-density sponge made for wet sanding. Saturate it with cool, clean water and wring it out just enough so it doesn't drip. Wipe joints and corners in the direction they run, and rinse the sponge frequently. Sponge sparingly, to avoid streaking.

Dust-free sanding systems come with both pole and hand sanding attachments that connect directly to your wet/dry vacuum or to a water filter that captures the bulk of the dust, keeping your vacuum filter clean.

Textures & Skim Coats

The most common texture on walls and ceilings is no texture at all. Smooth surfaces are easy to clean, are non-abrasive and are less likely to accumulate moisture, dirt and mold. And when the time comes, smooth surfaces are easy to repair and repaint. A coat of high-quality drywall primer, tinted to the color of the topcoat and sanded lightly with fine sandpaper, makes an adequate base for flat wall paint.

For a custom appearance, you can apply a skim coat of joint compound, which will make your wall resemble traditional plaster. Or, you can apply one of many textured finishes. For a basic skim coat, roll or spray a thinned drywall topping compound onto a properly taped and filled drywall surface and then scrape the surface smooth with a 12" trowel. A skim-coated surface is consistently smooth, and differences between the drywall paper and the dried joint compound are eliminated. This prevents taped joints and fastener patches from showing through paint. Skim coating is especially important under gloss paints and on surfaces that will be harshly lit.

Textured coatings have the advantage of being more forgiving of surface imperfections than paint alone. Most textures start with joint compound or, better, a joint-compound-like substance specially formulated for texturing. This "mud" may be thinned with water to a pancake-batter consistency for sprayer or roller application. Aggregates like sand or perlite may be included in the compound to create a gravelly texture. Applied mud may be left to dry or tooled to achieve a particular look.

Ceilings sprayed with popcorn texture contain vermiculite or polystyrene aggregates. Popcorn textures should not be used in contact areas, where aggregates may be scraped off. Aggregated textures may be left unpainted or spray-painted if desired (rollers tend to lift off the aggregate). If a somewhat washable aggregate surface is desired from the start, paints mixed with aggregates are available. Acoustical-rated ceiling textures have the best sound-deadening qualities.

Interesting textures involving swirls, patterns, or ridges add yet increased visual dimension to the surface of walls and ceilings. Thick and sharp textures should not be used where people may scrape against them, since peaks of plaster and sharp aggregates can cut through skin and catch clothing. Deep textures are also difficult to clean. Smooth, low textures such as orange peel and knock down are most appropriate for walls, since they are non-abrasive and are easy to paint and clean.

Ceiling and wall textures may be added to paint and rolled on or applied with a sprayer as a base coat for paint.

Applying a Skim Coat

Joint compound and drywall face paper have different porosities, which cause each to absorb paint and other decorative finishes differently. If taped walls and ceilings are not properly primed, seams and fastener heads can show through the finished paint job. This is called *photographing* and is readily apparent on surfaces that are under bright light or that are covered with high-gloss paint.

To combat photographing, apply a skim coat of thinned-down joint compound. A skim coat evens out surface textures to create a smooth, perfectly primed surface. Use all-purpose compound or drying-type topping compound for skim coating. Avoid setting-type compounds—if they dry too quickly they may not properly bond with the surface.

Tools & Materials ▸

Work gloves	Paint roller
Eye protection	12 to 14"
Particle mask	taping knife
Heavy-duty drill	Premixed all-purpose
with paddle mixer	or drying-type
5-gal. bucket	topping compound
Paint screen	Clean potable water
or roller pan	

Thin compound with cool water to a paint-like consistency, using a drill and mixing paddle. Pour compound into a roller tray. *Note: Use all-purpose compound or drying-type topping compound.*

Apply a thin coat of compound to the taped surface using a paint roller with a thin nap. Work in small sections so compound doesn't dry before you can smooth it.

Once a section is covered with compound, smooth the surface using a 12 to 14" taping knife. Work from the top down, applying enough pressure to leave a thin film of compound over the surface and remove ridges.

Preparing for Texture

Texturing does hide minor surface imperfections, but only to a point. Cracks larger than a hairline on old walls should be grooved, taped, and filled. New drywall should be taped, mudded, and sanded to a level 3 finish (see pages 62 to 63). Stains will bleed through texturing mud, so wash dirty or smoke-filmed walls with trisodium phosphate (TSP), then rinse and cover stains with an oil- or shellac-based, stain-blocking primer when the walls are dry.

Newly taped and finished drywall should be coated with drywall primers or flat latex wall paint, especially if textures will be tooled. Paint contains resins and fillers that help equalize the texture and porosity of mud- and paper-covered parts of the drywall. If you skip the paint step, texturing mud applied over taped joints will dry at a different rate than over drywall paper. Any tooling of this variable mud will leave the taped areas looking different than the field areas.

Texturing compounds are wet and heavy, which can lead to sagging ceilings as the drywall absorbs water from the texture and is pulled down by gravity. Make sure your drywall is thick enough for texture, given the spacing and orientation of the framing or furring (page 87). Keep materials and newly textured ceilings and walls above 55°F and well-ventilated until dry.

Protect nearby finished surfaces when applying textures. Spray equipment creates the most drift (overspray) and requires the most comprehensive masking. Rent or buy a dispenser that applies tape to one edge of 12" painter's paper as it is pulled off the roll. Tuck lightweight painter's plastic up under a mask edge of painter's paper and tape to the wall. A helper with a spray shield, essentially a 12 × 36" piece of plastic with a handle, is useful for protecting popcorn ceilings while spray-texturing walls. Unfinished drywall may be scraped smooth with a broad finishing knife while the compound is still wet.

Protect finished floors, fixtures, and already-finished walls and ceilings with drop cloths, masking paper, and painters plastic, as appropriate. Masking paper is a useful hybrid product that combines the full coverage and ease of application, but it does require a special applicator tool (see Resources on page 156).

Prime new drywall with flat latex wall paint or a primer/sealer specially formulated for new drywall (inset). Wash greasy or smoky painted surfaces with TSP and let dry, then prime stained areas with an oil-based stain-blocking primer. Dull glossy surfaces with sandpaper.

Preparation Options

Frame Spacing—Textured Gypsum Panel Ceilings* ▸

Board thickness in inches and type	Long edge of board relative to frame	Max. framing spacing o.c.
³⁄₈	Not recommended	–
½	Perpendicular only	16"
½ designated ceiling panels	Perpendicular only	24"
⅝	Perpendicular only	24"

*(from USG Gypsum Construction Handbook year 2000, page 196)

For wall applications, cover windows, doors, and any other openings with sheet plastic and painter's tape to seal around the edges. Make sure to cover all jambs as oversprayed texture can make trim installation more difficult.

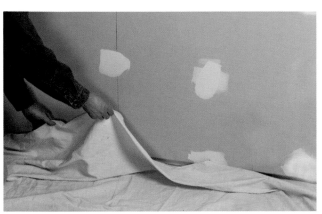

Use drop cloths to protect floors and for easy clean-up. Cover the entire floor area, overlapping drop cloths and sheet plastic protecting walls by 12".

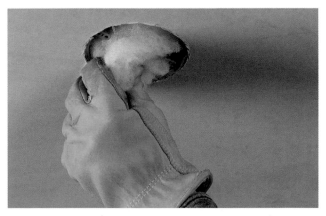

Stuff fiberglass insulation into electrical boxes and HVAC ducts to protect wiring and ducting.

Applying Textures

Textures may be applied with spray equipment, rollers, or trowels. These application methods create different looks. Spray equipment is expensive and requires some practice and skill to master. Still, spraying is the quickest application method, and equipment may be rented. Rolling is easy and safe and creates less mess, but is slower, does not work well with aggregated textures, and can be tricky on inside corners. Troweling is slower still, but works well for applying thick, smooth compound for deep texture effects.

When spraying or rolling, appropriate texturing compound is thinned to the consistency of pancake batter or thick paint. The best consistency is one that goes on smooth and doesn't run. Use trial and error on scrap drywall to find this point. Carefully record the water-to-compound ratio that produces the best results, and do not vary this during a job. Set spray equipment air pressure and use nozzle heads according to recommendations from the manufacturer or rental agency. Always test spray on scrap drywall to fine tune the pressure, and then keep the settings consistent throughout the job.

Apply compound or texture evenly. Before tooling rolled or sprayed surfaces, let the material dry for 10 to 15 minutes to a dull sheen. At this point, the surface can be textured with a dry roller, lightly knocked down with a large knife or trowel, or twisted, swirled, and stippled into any number of patterns with any number of instruments. Repeat a pattern in a meticulously measured and regular way or make completely random patterns. Avoid patterns that start off regular and then disintegrate.

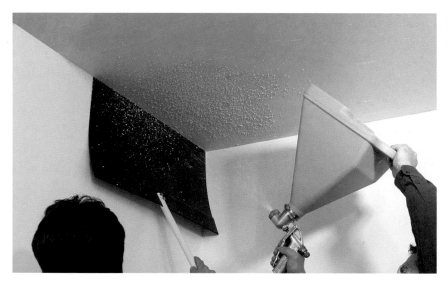

Use a spray shield to protect surfaces you don't want to receive texture during the texture application process.

Mix texture compound in a bucket using a joint-compound-mixing paddle mounted in a ½" drill. Follow the directions on the bag. Powdered compounds usually have a rest time that follows mixing before application may occur.

Applying a Popcorn Ceiling Texture

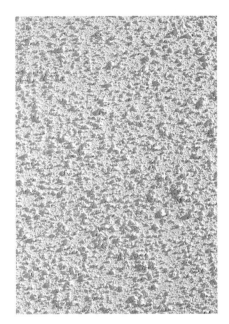

Popcorn texture is a popular treatment for ceilings. Its bumpy surface is created by tiny particles of vermiculite or polystyrene that give it sound-deadening properties. Mixtures are available in fine, medium, and coarse grades.

Mix the dry texture following the manufacturer's directions, then load the hopper of the texture gun. Apply the texture, holding the gun 2 to 4 ft. below the ceiling. Spray in a side-to-side motion (not arching), leaving a thin, even layer over the entire ceiling. Immediately following the first layer, spray on a second thin layer, working in a direction perpendicular to the first. Allow the texture to dry. For a heavy texture, the manufacturer may recommend applying an additional coat.

Applying an Orange Peel Texture

Orange peel textures are most commonly applied to walls. They have a distinctive, spattered look created by spraying a thin texturing product or water-thinned all-purpose drywall compound through a texturing gun. For a heavier spattered texture, repeat the step at right using less air pressure at the gun (atomizing air) and the compressor (feed pressure).

Mix the texture product or compound to the consistency of latex paint. Spray the surface with long, side-to-side strokes, keeping the gun perpendicular to the surface and about 18" away from it. To apply a heavy spatter-coat, let the surface dry for 10 to 15 minutes, then spray with random motions from about 6 ft. away.

Creating a Knock-down Texture

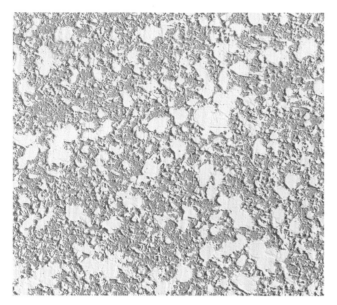

A knock-down texture is an orange peel texture that is partially smoothed with a drywall knife. Its relative flatness creates a subtle effect, and it's easier to paint and maintain than the heavier textures, making it a good choice for walls. Because of the light troweling required, this texture works best on smooth, flat surfaces.

Mix the texture product or all-purpose drywall compound to pancake batter consistency. Spray-texture the entire surface following the orange peel procedure on page 89. Let the texture dry for 10 to 15 minutes, then lightly trowel the surface with a 12" or larger drywall knife. Hold the knife almost flat, and work perpendicularly to the drywall seams.

Applying a Stipple Texture

Stipple textures are made with a paint roller and texture paint or all-purpose drywall compound. Randomly shaped ridges have a noticeable grain orientation. The amount of texture is affected by the nap of the roller, which can vary from ¼" to 1". Stippling can be knocked down for a flatter finish.

Mix paint or compound to a heavy latex-paint consistency. Coat the roller and roll the surface, recoating the roller as needed to create an even layer over the entire work area. Let the texture dry to a dull-wet sheen, then roll the surface again—without loading the roller—to create the finished texture.

Variation: Knock down the stipple finish for a smoother texture. Apply the stipple texture with a roller, and let it dry for about 10 minutes. Smooth the surface with a 12" or larger drywall knife, holding the knife almost flat and applying very light pressure.

Creating a Swirl Texture

Swirl textures and other freehand designs can have the look of traditionally applied plaster. Swirls can be made with a wallpaper brush, whisk broom, or any type of raking or combing tool.

Mix the texture product or all-purpose drywall compound to a heavy latex-paint consistency. For a shallow texture, use a paint roller with a ½" nap to apply an even coat over the entire surface; for a deeper texture, apply an even, ⅛"-thick coat with a drywall knife. Let the surface dry to a dull-wet appearance. Brush the pattern into the material using arching or circular motions. Start at one end of the area and work backward, overlapping the starting and end points of previous swirls with each new row.

Applying a Troweled Texture

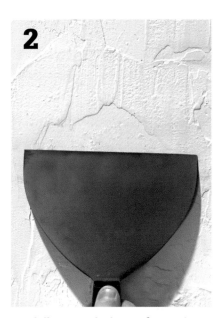

A troweled texture can have almost any design but should be applied with varied motions to create a random appearance. Premixed all-purpose drywall compound works well for most troweled textures, and it's usually best to work in small sections.

Apply the compound to the surface using a 6" or 8" drywall knife. Vary the direction of the strokes and the thickness of compound. If desired, stipple the surface by stamping the knife into the compound and pulling it away sharply.

Partially smooth the surface using a 6", 8" or 12" knife. Flatten the tops of ridges and stipples without smoothing lower areas. When you're satisfied with the design, repeat step 1 in an adjacent section, overlapping the edges of the textured area by a few inches.

Applying Veneer Plaster

While gypsum drywall all but wiped out traditional plaster and lath in the 1940s, a new generation of plaster products now make plaster easier and cheaper to apply, leading to new popularity for this classic material.

Veneer plaster systems provide a solid, uniform wall surface that is highly resistant to nail pops, cracks and surface damage. A skim coat of plaster is troweled onto a gypsum drywall base that has a distinctive blue color, commonly called *blueboard*. While blueboard is installed like standard drywall, it has a highly absorptive face paper to which the wet-mix plaster bonds. Blueboard joints do not need to be taped as precisely as standard drywall joints, and seams and fastener heads do not show through the finished plaster surface, a common problem with standard drywall.

Veneer systems are available in one-coat and two-coat systems. One-coat systems have a single layer of finish plaster applied directly to the blueboard base; two-coat systems employ a rough basecoat for the finish plaster to *key* or bond. Finish plaster can be troweled smooth or tooled for a texture. Sand and other additives can also be used to create coarser textures.

Applying veneer plaster effectively does take some time to master, but no more so than that of any masonry technique that requires troweling. The key is to apply the plaster in quick, short strokes, called *scratching in*, and then to immediately trowel it over with a steady, even stroke to smooth the plaster to a consistent thickness, typically ¹⁄₁₆ to ⅛".

Veneer plaster systems cost roughly 25 percent more to install than traditional drywall. However, veneer plaster can be installed in a single day, rather than the minimum of three days required for a drywall job. Additionally, veneer plaster does not need to be sanded, eliminating the additional setup and cleanup need for sanding drywall.

For best results, maintain a consistent room temperature during all phases of the plaster application until the material has dried completely. Plan your installation to allow for continuous application, from corner to corner, across a single surface. If you must stop partway through the application, use the trowel to cut a clean, sharp edge rather than feather out the coat. Do not overlap the applications, but rather use excess plaster to fill and bridge the joint during finish troweling.

Veneer plaster is highly resistant to surface damage, and can be installed in only one day.

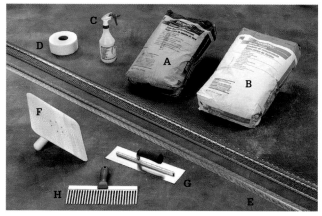

Tools and materials for installing veneer plaster include: dry-mix veneer plaster basecoats (A); finish plaster (B), available for smooth or textured applications; spray bottle for moistening surfaces (C); non-adhesive fiberglass mesh tape for covering blueboard panel seams and inside corners (D); outside corner beads with metal beads and mesh flanges (E); mortar hawk (F); 12" trowel (G); thin-wire rake for roughening the base coat (H).

Note: Each manufacturer has its own proprietary materials and methods for mixing, using, and applying veneer plaster systems. Always follow the detailed instructions provided by the manufacturer for the products you use.

Tools & Materials ▸

Work gloves
Eye protection
Stapler
Hammer
Heavy-duty ½" drill
    with mixing paddle

16-gal. drum
Mortar hawk
12" trowel
Thin-wire rake
    or broom
Spray water bottle

Metal corner bead
    with mesh flanges
1¼" drywall screws
Non-adhesive fiberglass
    mesh tape
¼" staples

Clean potable water
Dry-mix veneer
    basecoat plaster (for
    two-coat application)
Dry-mix veneer
    finish plaster

One- & Two-Coat Veneer Plaster Systems

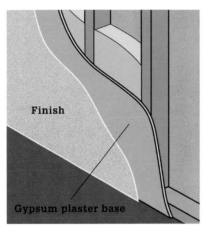

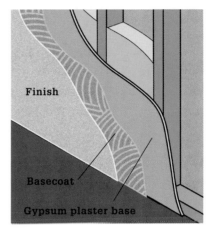

One-coat veneer plaster systems use a single, ¹⁄₁₆ to ³⁄₃₂"-thick coat of finish plaster applied directly to a blueboard base. The coat can be troweled smooth or textured, resulting in a hard, monolithic surface.

Two-coat veneer plaster systems are composed of a ¹⁄₁₆ to ⅛" basecoat plaster applied to blueboard, followed by a ¹⁄₁₆ to ³⁄₃₂"-thick coat of finish plaster. The finish coat bonds with the scratched basecoat surface, forming a more uniform and monolithic surface than that of a one-coat system.

Veneer Plaster Options

Veneer plaster can be troweled smooth or textured using standard techniques (see pages 94 to 97). As an alternative to paint, many manufacturers also offer pigment additives in a variety of colors. Scratches and other superficial flaws are therefore less noticeable, because the plaster itself is colored.

Other materials can be used as veneers to produce interesting walls and ceilings, such as concrete and clay. While most are applied using similar techniques to veneer plaster, always follow the manufacturer's instructions to achieve best results.

How to Finish Blueboard Seams with Mesh Tape

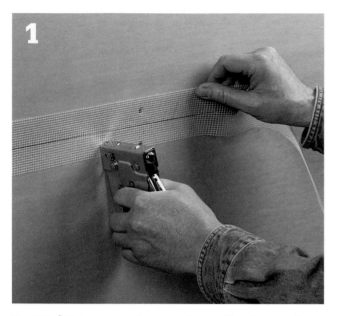

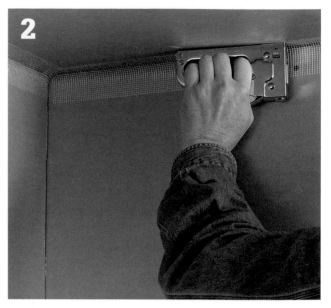

To tape flat seams, center non-adhesive fiberglass mesh tape over the joint and fasten at one end with two ¼" staples. Pull the tape taut across the joint and fasten the opposite end with two staples, then secure the tape with staples on alternate sides of the joint, every 24".

To tape inside corners, crease the tape in half lengthwise, and fasten to one surface only, with one staple at each end and then every 24" along the joint. At ceiling-to-wall joints, fasten tape to the ceiling-side; at wall-to-wall joints, fasten to either side. Avoid overlapping tape where possible. Install metal outside corner bead with mesh flanges as you would standard metal corner bead (see page 64).

How to Mix Veneer Plaster

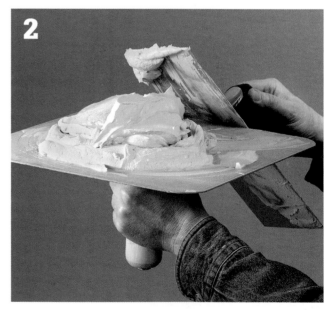

Following the manufacturer's instructions, mix one bag of dry plaster with the specified amount of clean, potable water in a 16-gal. smooth-sided container. To prevent accelerated set times, make sure all tools and containers are clean, and never add anything to the mix that is not specified by the manufacturer.

After all the plaster has been added, mix on high-speed for a couple minutes, stopping as soon as the plaster is smooth. Do not overmix plaster as it will decrease set time and reduce your trowel time. Clean mixing paddle and container immediately after use.

How to Apply a One-Coat Veneer Plaster System

Cover all seams. Apply a thin layer of plaster along all flat seams, feathering out the edges by 6". For inside corners, apply a thin bed of plaster and embed the loose side of the tape.

Variation: Blueboard joints can also be reinforced with paper tape. Embed the tape in a thin plaster bed, then cover with another thin layer to conceal the tape fully. *Note: Some manufacturers recommend setting-type compound for embedding paper tape; always follow the manufacturer's directions for the products you use.*

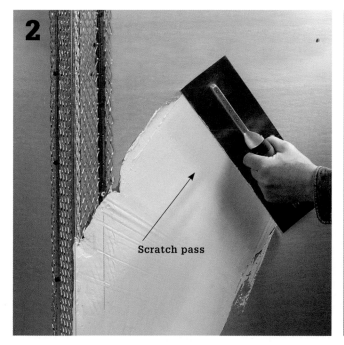

Scratch pass

Smooth pass

After the seams have set, begin plastering the surface, beginning at one corner and moving to the opposite. Start with ceilings and then do the walls, completing one entire surface before moving on to the next. To apply the plaster, tightly scratch-in the material up the wall (left), then immediately double-back over it, smoothing over the material to a thickness of ¹⁄₁₆ to ³⁄₃₂", as specified by the manufacturer (right). Use tight, quick strokes to apply the plaster during the scratch pass and long, even strokes to achieve consistency during the smooth pass.

(continued)

Continue to apply plaster by scratching in and smoothing over the surface. Don't worry about uniformity and trowel ridges at this point. Rather, make sure the entire surface is completely concealed with a relatively even plaster coat, ¹⁄₁₆ to ³⁄₃₂"-thick.

Once the plaster begins to firm (also called "taken up"), trowel the surface to fill any voids and remove tooling marks and imperfections, integrating the surface into a uniform smoothness.

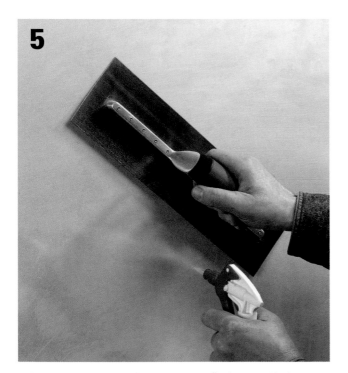

Prior to the plaster setting, make a final pass with the trowel to smooth the surface using water sparingly. Do not over-trowel; stop before the plaster begins to darken and sets.

Variation: For textured surfaces, skip the final troweling and work the surface with a texturing tool to achieve the desired results. See pages 88 to 91 for surface texturing techniques. *Note: Sand or texture added to the plaster mixture does not require tooling.*

How to Apply Basecoat in a Two-Coat Veneer Plaster System

1

2

Scratch pass   Smooth pass

Apply a thin layer of basecoat along all flat seams and corners, feathering out the edges by 6". For inside corners, apply a thin bed of basecoat and embed the loose tape, then cover with another thin layer. Allow all taped seams to set.

After the seams have set, tightly scratch in basecoat, then immediately double-back over it, smoothing over the material to a thickness of $\frac{1}{16}$ to $\frac{1}{8}$", as specified by the manufacturer. Use tight, quick strokes to apply basecoat for the scratch pass and long, even strokes to achieve consistency for the smooth pass.

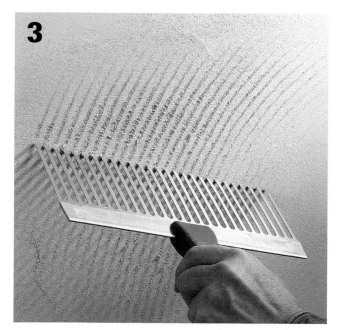

3

4

Once the plaster begins to firm or "take up," trowel the surface to fill any voids and remove tooling marks and imperfections, integrating the surface into a reasonably uniform surface—but don't over-trowel to a smooth surface. Then create keys for the final coat using a thin-wire rake to roughen the basecoat.

Approximately two hours after the basecoat has set, apply the finish coat using the same techniques as for a one-coat veneer plaster system (see pages 95 to 96).

Priming & Painting Drywall

Paints are either latex (water-based) or alkyd (oil-based). Latex paint is easy to apply and clean up, and the improved chemistry of today's latexes makes them suitable for nearly every application. Some painters feel that alkyd paint provides a smoother finish, but local regulations may restrict the use of alkyd products.

Paints come in various sheens, from high-gloss to flat. Gloss enamels dry to a shiny finish and are used for surfaces that need to be washed often, such as walls in bathrooms and kitchens and woodwork. Flat paints are used for most wall and ceiling applications.

Paint prices are typically an accurate reflection of quality. As a general rule, buy the best paint your budget can afford. High-quality paints are easier to use, look better, last longer, cover better, and because they often require fewer coats they are usually less expensive in the long run.

Before applying the finish paint, prime all of the surfaces with a good-quality primer. Primer bonds well to all surfaces and provides a durable base that keeps the paint from cracking and peeling. Priming is particularly important when using a high-gloss paint on walls and ceilings, because the paint alone might not completely hide finished drywall joints and other variations in the surface. To avoid the need for additional coats of expensive finish paint, tint the primer to match the new color.

How to Estimate Paint ▸

1) Length of wall or ceiling (linear feet)	×	
2) Height of wall, or width of ceiling	=	
3) Surface area (square feet)	÷	
4) Coverage per gallon of chosen paint	=	
5) Gallons of paint needed		

For large jobs, mix paint together (called "boxing") in a large pail to eliminate slight color variations between cans. Stir the paint thoroughly with a wooden stick or power drill attachment.

Latex-based drywall primer and sealer equalizes the absorption rates between the dried joint compound and the drywall paper facing, allowing the paint to go on evenly with no blotching.

Selecting a Quality Paint

Paint coverage (listed on can labels) of quality paint should be about 400 square feet per gallon. Bargain paints (left) may require two or even three coats to cover the same area as quality paints (right).

High washability is a feature of quality paint. The pigments in bargain paints (right) may "chalk" and wash away with mild scrubbing.

Paint Sheens

Paint comes in a variety of surface finishes, or sheens. Gloss enamel (A) provides a highly reflective finish for areas where high washability is important. All gloss paints tend to show surface flaws. Alkyd-base enamels have the highest gloss. Medium-gloss (or "satin") latex enamel (B) creates a highly washable surface with a slightly less reflective finish. Like gloss enamels, medium-gloss paints tend to show surface flaws. Eggshell enamel (C) combines a soft finish with the washability of enamel. Flat latex (D) is an all-purpose paint with a matte finish that hides surface irregularities.

Painting Tools

Most painting jobs can be completed with a few quality tools. Purchase two or three premium brushes, a sturdy paint pan that can be attached to a stepladder and one or two good rollers. With proper cleanup, these tools will last for years. See pages 102 to 103 for tips on how to use paintbrushes and rollers.

Choosing a Paintbrush

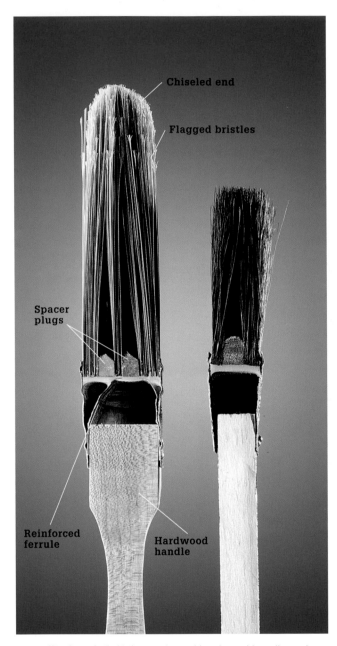

A quality brush (left), has a shaped hardwood handle and a sturdy, reinforced ferrule made of noncorrosive metal. Multiple spacer plugs separate the bristles. A quality brush has flagged (split) bristles and a chiseled end for precise edging. A cheaper brush (right) will have a blunt end, unflagged bristles, and a cardboard spacer plug that may soften when wet.

There's a proper brush for every job. A 4" straight-edged brush (bottom) is good for cutting in along ceilings and corners. For woodwork, a 2" trim brush (middle) works well. A tapered sash brush (top) helps with corners. Use brushes made of natural bristles only with alkyd paints. All-purpose brushes, suitable for all paints, are made with a blend of polyester, nylon, and sometimes natural bristles.

Choosing Paint Rollers

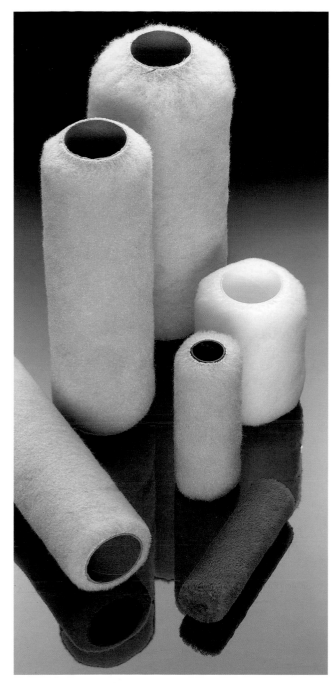

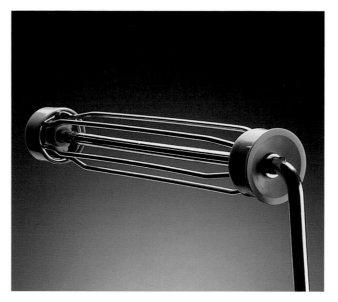

Choose a sturdy roller with a wire cage construction. Nylon bearings should roll smoothly and easily when you spin the cage. The handle end should be threaded for attaching an extension handle.

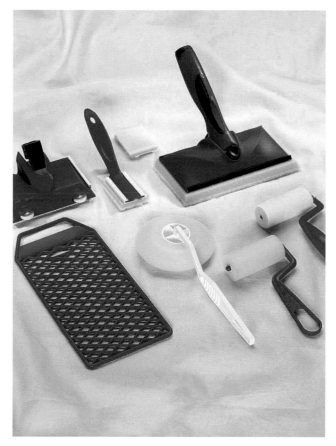

Select the proper roller cover for the surface you intend to paint. A ¼"-nap cover is used for enamel paints and very flat surfaces. A ⅜"-nap cover will hide the small flaws found in most flat walls and ceilings. A 1"-nap cover is for rough surfaces like concrete blocks or stucco. Foam rollers fit into small spaces and work well when painting furniture or doing touch-ups. Corner rollers have nap on the ends and make it easy to paint corners without cutting in the edges. Synthetic covers are good with most paints, especially latexes. Wool or mohair roller covers give an even finish with alkyd products. Always choose good-quality roller covers, which will be less likely to shed lint.

Paint pads and specialty rollers come in a wide range of sizes and shapes to fit different painting needs.

Painting Walls & Ceilings

For a smooth finish on large wall and ceiling areas, paint in small sections. First use a paintbrush to cut in the edges, then immediately roll the section before moving on. If brushed edges are left to dry before the large surfaces are rolled, visible lap marks will be left on the finished wall. Working in natural light makes it easier to see missed areas.

Spread the paint evenly onto the work surface without letting it run, drip or lap onto other areas. Excess paint will run on the surface and can drip onto woodwork and floors. Conversely, stretching paint too far leaves lap marks and results in patchy coverage.

For fast, mess-free painting, shield any surfaces that could get splattered. If you are painting only the ceiling, drape the walls and woodwork to prevent splatters. When painting walls, mask the baseboards and the window and door casings. (See top of opposite page.)

While the tried-and-true method of aligning painter's tape with the edge of moldings and casings is perfectly adequate, the job goes much faster and smoother with a tape applicator. Similarly, painter's tape can be used to cover door hinges and window glass, but hinge masks and corner masks simplify the job enormously. Evaluate the available choices and the project at hand: there are many new, easy-to-use options available.

Use an adjustable extension handle to paint ceilings and tall walls easily without a ladder.

Cut in around doors and window casing with a paintbrush and then finish painting the wall with a roller.

How to Tape and Drape for Walls and Ceilings

1

Align wide masking tape with the inside edge of the molding; press in place. Run the tip of a putty knife along the inside edge of the tape to seal it against seeping paint. After painting, remove the tape as soon as the paint is too dry to run.

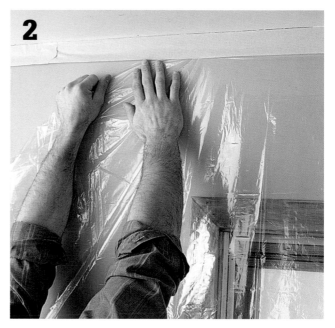

2

Press the top half of 2" masking tape along the joint between the ceiling and the wall, leaving the bottom half of the tape loose. Hang sheet plastic under the tape, draping the walls and baseboards. After painting, remove the tape as soon as the paint is too dry to run.

Specialized Roller Techniques ▸

Using a corner roller makes it unnecessary to cut in inside corners. It also matches the rolled texture of the rest of the wall better than most paint brushes.

Minimize brush marks. Slide the roller cover slightly off of the roller cage when rolling near wall corners or a ceiling line. Brushed areas dry to a different finish than rolled paint.

Curved Walls

Curved walls have obvious appeal and are surprisingly easy to build. Structurally, a curved wall is very similar to a standard nonload-bearing partition wall, with two key differences: the stud spacing and the materials used for the top and bottom wall plates.

Traditionally, plates for curved walls were cut from ¾" plywood—a somewhat time-consuming and wasteful process—but now a flexible track product made of light-gauge steel has made the construction much easier (see Resources, page 156). Using the steel track, frame the wall based on a layout drawn onto the floor. Shape the track to follow the layout, screw together the track pieces to lock-in the shape, then add the studs.

The ideal stud spacing for your project depends upon the type of finish material you plan to use. If it's drywall, ¼" flexible panels (usually installed in double layers) require studs spaced a maximum of 9" O.C. for curves with a minimum radius of 32". For radii less than 32", you may have to wet the panels.

By virtue of their shape, curved walls provide some of their own stability. Half-walls with pronounced curves may not need additional support if they're secured at one end. If your wall needs additional support, look for ways to tie it into the existing framing, or install cabinets or other permanent fixtures for stability.

If you are planning a curved wall of full height, use a plumb bob to transfer the layout of the bottom track up to the ceiling for the layout of the top track. Check the alignment by placing a few studs at the ends and middle, and then fasten the top track to the ceiling joists with drywall screws.

When hanging drywall on curved walls, it's best to install the panels perpendicular to the framing. Try to avoid joints, but if they are unavoidable, note that vertical seams are much easier to hide in the curve than horizontal seams. If panels have been wetted for the installation, allow them to dry thoroughly before taping seams.

Cutting Standard Steel Tracks ▸

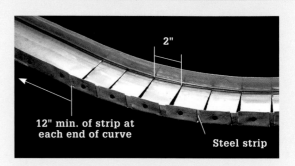

2"

12" min. of strip at each end of curve

Steel strip

As a substitute for flexible track, use standard 20- or 25-gauge steel track. Along the curved portion of the wall, cut the web and flange along the outside of the curve at 2" intervals. From the web of a scrap piece, cut a 1"-wide strip that runs the length of the curve, plus 8". Bend the track to follow the curve, then screw the strip to the inside of the outer flange, using 7/16" Type S screws. This construction requires 12" of straight (uncut) track at both ends of the curve.

A curved wall can be created in several ways using traditional framing and drywall methods or modern products that eliminate much of the work.

How to Frame a Curved Wall

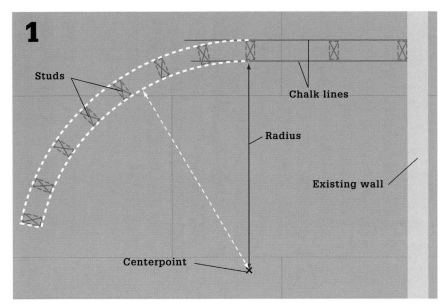

Draw the wall layout. Mark straight portions with parallel chalk lines representing the outside edges of the wall track. Use a framing square to make sure the lines are perpendicular to the adjoining wall. At the start of the curve, square off from the chalk line and measure out the distance of the radius to mark the curve's centerpoint. For small curves (4 ft., or so), drive a nail at the centerpoint, hook the end of a tape measure on the nail, and draw the curve using the tape and a pencil as a compass; for larger curves, use a straight board nailed at the centerpoint.

Position the track along the layout lines, following the curve exactly. Mark the end of the wall onto the track using a marker, then cut the track to length with aviation snips. Cut the top track to the same length.

Reposition the bottom track on the layout, then apply masking tape along the outside flanges. Secure the track by driving a Type S screw through each flange and into the strap. Screw both sides of the track. Turn over the bottom track, then set the top track on top and match its shape. Tape and screw the top track.

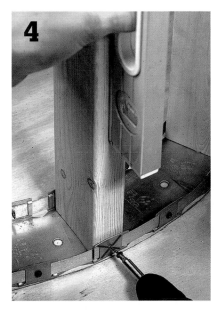

Fasten the bottom track to the floor, using 1¼" drywall screws. Mark the stud layout onto both tracks. Cut the studs to length. Install the studs one at a time, using a level to plumb each along its narrow edge, then driving a 1¼" screw through the flange or strap and into the stud on both sides.

Fit the top track over the studs and align them with the layout marks. Fasten the studs to the top track with one screw on each side, checking the wall for level and height as you work. Set the level on top of the track, both parallel and perpendicular to the track, before fastening each stud.

Installing Drywall on Curves

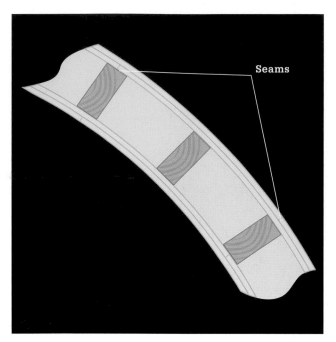

Use two layers of ¼" flexible drywall for curved walls and arches. If there are butted seams, stagger the seams between layers.

Install corner bead with adhesive and staples or drywall nails. Do not use screws to attach corner bead—they will cause the bead material to kink and distort.

Hanging Flexible Drywall

Start at the center for concave curves. Cut the first panel a little long and position it lengthwise along the wall. Carefully bend the panel toward the midpoint of the curve and fasten it to the center stud. Work toward the ends to fasten the rest of the panel. Install the second panel over the first, then trim along the top of the wall with a drywall saw.

Start at one end for convex curves. Cut the panel long and fasten it lengthwise along the wall, bending the panel as you work. Add the second layer, then trim both to the framing. To cover the top of a curved wall, set a ½" panel on the wall and scribe it from below.

Hanging Drywall in Archways

Cut ¼" flexible drywall to width and a few inches longer then needed. Fasten to the arch with 1¼" drywall screws, working from the center out to the ends. Trim the ends of the piece and install a second to match the thickness of the surrounding drywall.

Variation: Score the backside of ½" drywall every inch (or more for tighter curves) along the length of the piece. Starting at one end, fasten the piece along the arch; the scored drywall will conform to the arch.

Wet-bending ▸

Drywall is relatively easy to conform to surfaces that curve in just one direction, as long as you wet the tensioned surface of the drywall and don't try to bend it farther than it will go. When wetted and rested for an hour, ½" drywall will bend to a 4 ft. radius, ⅜" to a 3 ft. radius, and ¼" to a 2 ft. radius. Special flexible ¼" drywall does not require wetting for radii greater than 32".

Set framing members closer together for curved surfaces to avoid flat spots. Radii less than 5 ft. require 12" frame spacing, less than 4 ft. require 8" spacing, and less than 3 ft. require 6" spacing. Hang the factory edge of panels perpendicular to the framing so the panels bend longwise. ¼" panels should be doubled up; stagger the panels so no joints line up.

Wet the side of the panel that will be stretched by the bend with about 1 quart of water using a paint roller. Cover the panel with plastic or face the wet sides of two sheets of drywall toward each other and let sit for 1 hour before application.

Architectural Details

Drywall can be installed in layers or in conjunction with a 2× framework to bring a wide variety of architectural detail to a room. From a simple series of tiers wrapping the perimeter of a room (shown here) to curved soffits or raised panels on walls, you can replicate designs you've seen in high-end homes or bring your own creation to life.

The same basic technique used to hang drywall in multiple layers applies to adding built-up drywall detail. Use a sharp utility knife and a rasp for cutting as panel edges must be clean for finishing. The use of adhesive is highly recommended to create strong bonds between layers so the pieces hold together tightly. Use Type G screws to hold panels together while the adhesive sets up. Use L-bead to create sharp, clean panel ends. Finish all seams and beads with joint tape and at least three coats of compound, following standard finishing techniques.

See pages 128 to 129 for more information on installing drywall in multiple layers.

Tools & Materials ▸

Work gloves	Screwgun or ⅜" drill
Eye protection	Drywall
Tape measure	Drywall screws
T-square	L-bead
Utility knife	Adhesive
Chalk line	Joint compound

Add architectural detail to walls and ceilings by building up decorative layers of drywall.

Creating Built-up Drywall Details ▸

For a more substantial step soffit, build a 2× framework as a base for the drywall. As you lay out the placement of the new framing, make sure to account for the thickness of the drywall in all final dimensions.

How to Add Decorative Tiers to a Ceiling

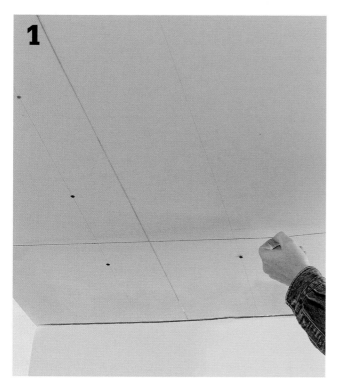

Measure and mark the width of the first tier on the ceiling along each wall, then snap chalk lines to mark the perimeter.

Cut pieces of drywall to size, apply ⅜" beads of adhesive to the backside and install with drywall screws, following the spacing chart on page 17.

Snap chalk lines for the second tier, then cut and install the drywall as described in step 2. Stagger all seams at corners and along tiera runs.

Install L-bead on all exposed edges of each tier, then finish with three coats of joint compound. Edges can also be finished with flexible corner tape.

Garage Drywall

Whether or not to install finished interior walls on your garage is mostly a matter of preference. The only time wall surfaces are required is when your garage shares a wall with your house (an attached garage) or if one of the walls in your detached garage runs parallel to the house and is constructed within 3 feet of the house. In both cases, only the shared or closest walls need to be finished to block the spreading of fire. Typically, a wallcovering of ½"-thick (minimum) drywall with taped seams is required. Some circumstances may demand that you install fire-rated, Type X drywall or a double layer of drywall. The seams between drywall panels on fireblocking walls must be finished with tape embedded in joint compound or with adhesive-backed fireblocking tape.

If the area above the garage is occupied by a habitable room, the garage walls should be covered with ½" drywall to provide rigidity and structure and the ceiling should be finished with ⅝"-thick Type X drywall. Ceiling seams should be covered with tape and compound. Fastener heads do not need to be covered with compound except for visual reasons.

If your goal is to create a garage with walls that are finished to interior standards or serve to prevent fire spreading, then drywall is an excellent wallcovering. Although the price and availability of diverse building materials fluctuates rather dramatically, drywall is typically one of the more economical choices. But because drywall is relatively susceptible to damage from impact (for example, from tools or bicycles) and doesn't withstand exposure to moisture well, many homeowners choose other wallcoverings for their garage. Exterior siding panels are thick enough to hold fasteners and withstand moisture well, but are relatively costly and most have a rougher texture that can be bothersome on interior spaces. Interior paneling has only minimal structural value, but it may be more visually pleasing to you and some styles are fairly inexpensive.

Plywood and oriented strand-board (OSB) are popular products for garage walls. Thicker panels (½ to ¾" thick) give excellent rigidity to the walls and are suitable for holding some fasteners. They can be left unfinished, clear-coated for protection with polyurethane finish (or comparable), or you may choose to paint them. A lighter colored wall paint in semi-gloss or gloss is a good choice. Sheet goods that have a pleasing color or woodgrain may be finished with either a clear coating or a protective deck/siding stain. Lauan plywood underlayment, for example, has a natural mahogany color that can be pleasing when treated with a reddish exterior stain or clear coat. It is also inexpensive but it is thin (roughly ¼") and can only support very light-duty fasteners with little load, such as a stickpin holding a wall calendar.

Finishing your garage walls with drywall or other panel products improves the appearance of your garage and also can serve practical functions such as forming a fireblock or concealing wiring or plumbing.

How to Hang Drywall in a Garage

Begin installing drywall panels in a corner. You can install the panels vertically or horizontally, depending on the wall height and how much cutting is involved. Unlike interior walls, garage walls are seldom a standard 8 ft. If you are finishing a ceiling with drywall, cover the ceiling first so you can press the tops of the wall panels up against the ceiling panels. This helps support the ends of the ceiling panels. Drive coarse 1¼" drywall screws every 16".

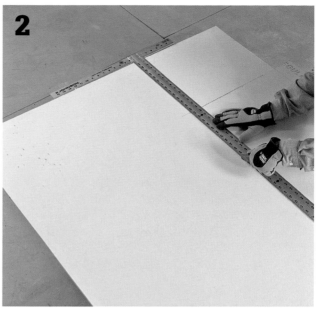

Cut drywall pieces to fit around doors and windows. Take special care if you are covering a firewall since any gaps will need to be filled with joint compound and taped over. Make straight cuts that run full width or length by scoring through the face paper with a utility knife and then snapping along the scored line. Finish the cut by slicing through the paper of the back face.

Mark and make cutouts for electrical and utility boxes. Use a drywall saw, keyhole saw or spiral saw to make the cutouts. Make sure the front edges of the boxes are flush with the face of the drywall (move the boxes or add mud rings, if necessary). Finish installing all panels.

Cover seams between drywall panels with joint compound; use drywall tape on walls that serve as firewalls. Cover tape with two layers of feathered-out joint compound, and then cover all fastener heads if you will be painting the walls. Give the panels a coat of drywall primer before painting.

Framed Soffits

A soffit is a structure that hangs down from a ceiling or overhang, usually filling the cornice area where the wall meets the ceiling. In your kitchen you may choose to install soffits above wall cabinets to create a solid wall surface. You may want to add a soffit to conceal the ductwork from an exhaust fan. Or, you might use a soffit to create a visual barrier (as well as a barrier to airborne food particles, odors, and grease) between kitchen and dining areas in an open floor plan. Soffits are also great for hiding recessed lighting fixtures if it is not possible to install recessed lighting in the existing ceiling.

If you are installing new cabinets, the soffits need to be built and installed first. That means you need to do the cabinet layout on the walls, then construct the soffits, taking care to make them level and plumb. Soffits above cabinets may be flush with the cabinets, extend a few inches for a slight visual reveal, or extend farther (at least 8") to accommodate canister light fixtures.

Tools & Materials ▸

Work gloves	6, 8, and 10"
Eye protection	mudding knives
Tape measure	Drywall compound
Chalk line	Carpenter's square
Level	Table saw
Stud finder	Lighting or ductwork
Lumber	Hammer
(2 × 2, 2 × 4)	Drywall tape
2½" screws	(if desired)
⅝" drywall	Sandpaper
Drywall screws	Primer and paint
Cordless drill	
Utility knife	

How to Install a Soffit

Mark the desired outline of the soffits onto the ceiling. Use a carpenter's square to mark square corners. Use a chalk line to mark long straight sections. Use a stud finder to locate the ceiling joists and wall studs in the area of the soffits.

Build a ladder-like framework of 2 × 2s for the soffit sides. If you cannot find straight 2 × 2s, use a table saw to rip 2 × 4s in half. Attach the crossbars at regular intervals of 16 or 24" on center using 2½" screws. Create the ladder so the crossbars will not be aligned with the ceiling joists and wall studs when the framework is installed.

If the joists are perpendicular to the soffit, screw the soffit framework to the joists, aligned with the chalk lines. If not, go to the next step.

If the joists are parallel to the soffit location, cut 2 × 4s to a length 1½" shorter than the width of the soffit. Screw these boards into the ceiling joists and toe-screw the ends into the ceiling wall plate.

Attach the soffit framework to the ends of the 2 × 4s with drywall screws.

Use a level or laser level to mark the wall even with the bottom of the installed soffit framework. Cut 2 × 2s to the length of the soffit and attach this cleat to the wall aligned with the mark.

Cut crossmembers to fit between the bottom of the framework and the wall cleat. Attach the crossmembers by toe-screwing into the cleat and end-screwing through the framework side. Place the crossmembers every 16" on center.

Install lighting or ductwork, if needed. Extend the mounting bars on recessed fixtures to reach framing members. Finish installing lights, and then check to make sure they work. Once you've determined that the lights work properly, have the work inspected by an electrician and/or a local building inspector. With approval, you can begin to close up the soffit.

Cut and install ⅝" drywall over the framework using drywall screws. Attach the bottom sections first, then cut and attach the sides. *Note: Required minimum drywall thickness is dictated by local building codes. Be sure to consult them before you begin installation.*

Apply joint compound and tape to the drywall. Use corner tape along all the edges. Sand smooth and finish with primer and paint.

Basement Prep: Solution 1

As a general rule, avoid insulating the interior side of your basement walls. It is best to leave breathing space for the concrete or block so moisture that enters through the walls is not trapped. If your basement walls stay dry and show no signs of dampness, however, adding some interior insulation can increase the comfort level in your basement. If you are building a stud wall for hanging wallcovering materials, you can insulate between the studs with rigid foam—do not use fiberglass batts and do not install a vapor barrier. If you are building a stud wall, it's a good idea to keep the wall away from the basement wall so there is an air channel between the two.

Interior insulation can be installed in the basement if your foundation walls are dry. It is important to keep the framed wall isolated from the basement wall with a seamless layer of rigid insulation board.

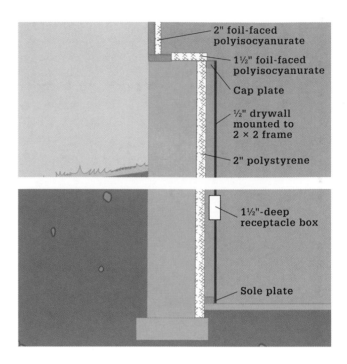

2" foil-faced polyisocyanurate

1½" foil-faced polyisocyanurate

Cap plate

½" drywall mounted to 2 × 2 frame

2" polystyrene

1½"-deep receptacle box

Sole plate

How to Insulate an Interior Basement Wall

1

Begin on the exterior wall by digging a trench and installing a 2"-thick rigid foam insulation board up to the bottom of the siding and down at least 6" below grade. The main purpose of this insulation is to inhibit convection and air transfer in the wall above grade.

2

Insulate the rim joist with strips of 2"-thick isocyanurate rigid insulation with foil facing. Be sure the insulation you purchase is rated for interior exposure (exterior products can produce bad vapors). Use adhesive to bond the insulation to the rim joist, and then caulk around all the edges with acoustic sealant.

Seal and insulate the top of the foundation wall, if it is exposed, with strips of 1½"-thick, foil-faced isocyanurate insulation. Install the strips using the same type of adhesive and caulk you used for the rim joist insulation.

Attach sheets of 2"-thick extruded polystyrene insulation to the wall from the floor to the top of the wall. Make sure to clean the wall thoroughly and let it dry completely before installing the insulation.

Seal the gaps between the insulation boards with insulation vapor barrier tape. Do not caulk gaps between the insulation boards and the floor.

Install a stud wall by fastening the cap plate to the ceiling joists and the sole plate to the floor. If you have space, allow an air channel between the studs and the insulation. Do not install a vapor barrier.

Basement Prep: Solution 2

Wall framing members can be attached directly to a concrete foundation wall to provide a support for wall coverings and to house wires and pipes. Because they have no significant structural purpose, they are usually made with smaller stock called furring strips, which can be 2 × 2 or 2 × 3 wood. Do not install furring strips in conjunction with a vapor barrier or insulation, and do not attach them to walls that are not dry walls, with insulation on the exterior side.

Furring strips serve primarily to create nailing surfaces for drywall. Attach them to dry basement walls at web locations of block wall where possible.

How to Attach Furring Strips to Dry Foundation Walls

Cut a 2 × 2 top plate to span the length of the wall. Mark the furring-strip layout onto the bottom edge of the plate using 16" O.C. spacing. Attach the plate to the bottom of the joists with 2½" drywall screws. The back edge of the plate should line up with the front of the blocks.

If the joists run parallel to the wall, you'll need to install backers between the outer joist and the sill plate to provide support for ceiling drywall. Make T-shaped backers from short 2 × 4s and 2 × 2s. Install each so the bottom face of the 2 × 4 is flush with the bottom edge of the joists. Attach the top plate to the foundation wall with its top edge flush with the top of the blocks.

Install a bottom plate cut from pressure-treated 2 × 2 lumber so the plate spans the length of the wall. Apply construction adhesive to the back and bottom of the plate, then attach it to the floor with a nailer. Use a plumb bob to transfer the furring-strip layout marks from the top plate to the bottom plate.

Cut 2 × 2 furring strips to fit between the top and bottom plates. Apply construction adhesive to the back of each furring strip, and position it on the layout marks on the plates. Nail along the length of each strip at 16" intervals.

Option: Leave a channel for the installation of wires or supply pipes by installing pairs of vertically aligned furring strips with a 2" gap between each pair. *Note: Consult local codes to ensure proper installation of electrical or plumbing materials.*

Isolate the Wall ▶

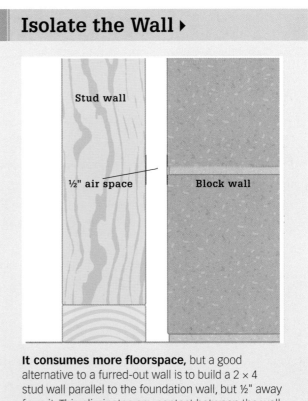

Stud wall

½" air space

Block wall

It consumes more floorspace, but a good alternative to a furred-out wall is to build a 2 × 4 stud wall parallel to the foundation wall, but ½" away from it. This eliminates any contact between the wall framing members and the foundation wall.

Soundproofing

In making homes quieter, building professionals add soundproofing elements to combat everything from the hum of appliances to the roar of airliners. Many of the techniques they use are simple improvements involving common products and materials. What will work best in your home depends upon a few factors, including the types of noises involved, your home's construction and how much remodeling you have planned. For starters, it helps to know a little of the science behind sound control.

Sound is created by vibrations traveling through air. Consequently, the best ways to reduce sound transmission are by limiting airflow and blocking or absorbing vibrations. Effective soundproofing typically involves a combination of methods.

Stopping airflow—through walls, ceilings, floors, windows, and doors—is essential to any soundproofing effort. (Even a 2-ft.-thick brick wall would not be very soundproof if it had cracks in the mortar.) It's also the simplest way to make minor improvements. Because you're dealing with air, this kind of soundproofing is a lot like weatherizing your home: add weatherstripping and door sweeps, seal air leaks with caulk, install storm doors and windows, etc. The same techniques that keep out the cold also block exterior noise and prevent sound from traveling between rooms.

After reducing airflow, the next level of soundproofing is to improve the sound-blocking qualities of your walls and ceilings. Engineers rate soundproofing performance of wall and ceiling

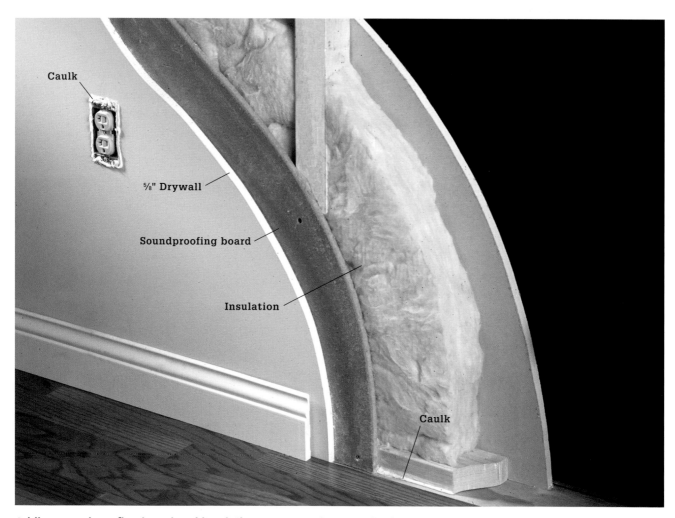

Caulk

⅝" Drywall

Soundproofing board

Insulation

Caulk

Adding soundproofing board and insulation are among the many simple ways you can reduce noise in your home.

STC Ratings for Various Wall & Ceiling Constructions* ▶

Assembly	STC Rating
Wood-frame Walls	
2 × 4 wall; ½" drywall on both sides; no caulk	30
2 × 4 wall; ½" drywall on both sides; caulked	35
2 × 4 wall; ½" drywall on both sides; additional layer of ⅝" fire-resistant drywall on one side	38
2 × 4 wall; ½" drywall on both sides; additional layer of ⅝" fire-resistant drywall on both sides	40
2 × 4 wall; ½" drywall on both sides; insulated	39
Staggered-stud 2 × 4 wall; ⅝" fire-resistant drywall on each side; insulated	50
2 × 4 wall, soundproofing board (base layer) and ⅝" fire-resistant drywall on each side; insulated	50
2 × 4 wall with resilient steel channels on one side; ⅝" fire-resistant drywall on both sides; insulated	52
Steel-frame Walls	
3⅝" metal studs, spaced 24" on-center; ⅝" fire-resistant drywall on both sides	40
3⅝" metal studs, spaced 24" on-center; ½" fire-resistant drywall single layer on one side, doubled on other side; insulated	48
2½" metal studs, spaced 24" on-center; soundproofing board (base layer) and ½" fire-resistant drywall on both sides; insulated	50
Wood-frame Floor/Ceiling	
Drywall below; subfloor and resilient (vinyl) flooring above	32
⅝" fire-resistant drywall attached to resilient steel channels below; subfloor, pad, and carpet above	48
Double layer ⅝" fire-resistant drywall attached to resilient steel channels below; subfloor, pad, and carpet above	Up to 60

*All assemblies are sealed with caulk, except where noted. Ratings are approximate.

assemblies using a system called Sound Transmission Class, or STC. The higher the STC rating, the more sound is blocked by the assembly. For example, if a wall is rated at 30 to 35 STC, loud speech can be understood through the wall. At 42 STC, loud speech is reduced to a murmur. At 50 STC, loud speech cannot be heard through the wall.

Standard construction methods typically result in a 28 to 32 STC rating, while soundproofed walls and ceilings can carry ratings near 50. To give you an idea of how much soundproofing you need, a sleeping room at 40 to 50 STC is quiet enough for most people; a reading room is comfortable at 35 to 40 STC. For another gauge, consider the fact that increasing the STC rating of an assembly by 10 reduces the perceived sound levels by 50 percent. The chart above lists the STC ratings of several wall and ceiling assemblies.

Improvements to walls and ceilings usually involve increasing the mass, absorbancy, or resiliency of the assembly; often, a combination is best. Adding layers of drywall increases mass, helping a wall resist the vibrational force of sound (⅝" fire-resistant drywall works best because of its greater weight and density). Insulation and soundproofing board absorb sound. Soundproofing board is available through drywall suppliers and manufacturers (see page 156). Some board products are gypsum-based; others are lightweight fiberboard. Installing resilient steel channels over the framing or old surface and adding a new layer of drywall increases mass, while the channels allow the surface to move slightly and absorb vibrations. New walls built with staggered studs and insulation are highly effective at reducing vibration.

In addition to these permanent improvements, you can reduce noise by decorating with soft materials that absorb sound. Rugs and carpet, drapery, fabric wall hangings and soft furniture help reduce atmospheric noise within a room. Acoustical ceiling tiles effectively absorb and help contain sound within a room but do little to prevent sound from entering the room.

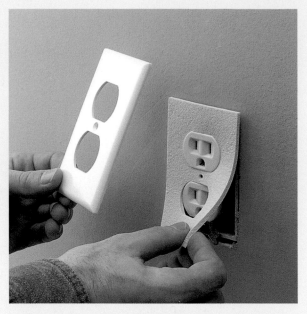

Stop airflow between rooms by sealing the joints where walls meet floors. With finished walls, remove the shoe molding and spray insulating foam, acoustic sealant, or non-hardening caulk under the baseboards. Also seal around door casings. With new walls, seal along the top and bottom plates.

Cover switch and receptacle boxes with foam gaskets to prevent air leaks. Otherwise, seal around the box perimeter with acoustic sealant or caulk and seal around the knockout where the cables enter the box.

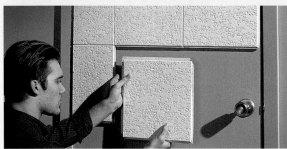

Soundproof doors between rooms by adding a sweep at the bottom and weatherstripping along the stops. If doors are hollow-core, replacing them with solid-core units will increase soundproofing performance. Soundproof workshop and utility room doors with a layer of acoustical tiles.

Reduce sound transmission through ductwork by lining ducts with special insulation. If a duct supplying a quiet room has a takeoff point close to that of a noisy room, move one or both ducts so their takeoff points are as distant from each other as possible.

Installing Resilient Steel Channels

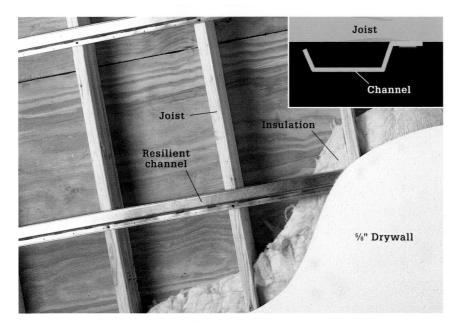

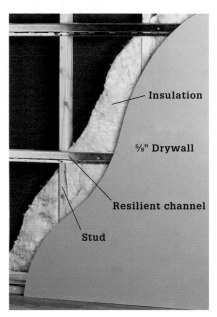

On ceilings, install channels perpendicular to the joists, spaced 24" on-center. Fasten at each joist with 1¼" Type W drywall screws, driven through the channel flange. Stop the channels 1" short of all walls. Join pieces on long runs by overlapping the ends and fastening through both pieces. Insulate the joist bays with unfaced fiberglass or other insulation and install ⅝" fire-resistant drywall, perpendicular to the channels. For double-layer application, install the second layer of drywall perpendicular to the first.

On walls, use the same installation techniques as with the ceiling application, installing the channels horizontally. Position the bottom channel 2" from the floor and the top channel within 6" of the ceiling. Insulate the stud cavities and install the drywall vertically.

How to Build Staggered-stud Partition Walls

Frame new partition walls using 2 × 6 plates. Space the studs 12" apart, staggering them so alternate studs are aligned with opposite sides of the plates. Seal under and above the plates with acoustic sealant.

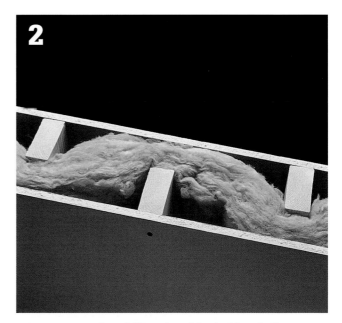

Weave R-11 unfaced fiberglass blanket insulation horizontally between the studs. Cover each side with one or more layers of ⅝" fire-resistant drywall.

Multiple Drywall Layers

Installing drywall in multiple layers is an effective means of soundproofing and also increases the fire-rating of walls and ceilings. Drywall can be heavy, especially when installed in layers, so it's important to install panels correctly to prevent sagging, cracks, and popped fasteners. Always fasten both the base layer (which can be standard drywall or a soundproofing board) and the face layer with the correct number of screws (see page 47). Panels can be secured with fasteners alone, though many manufacturers recommend the use of panel adhesive. It's best to install the base layer vertically and the face layer horizontally, staggering the joints. If panels must be hung in the same direction, stagger parallel seams between layers by at least 10"

See pages 124 to 127 for more on soundproofing walls and ceilings.

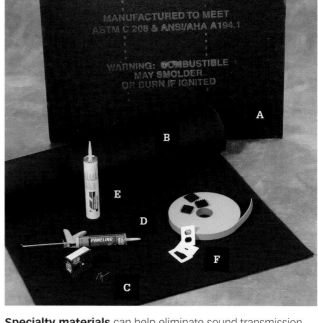

Specialty materials can help eliminate sound transmission better than drywall alone. High-density gypsum and cellulose fiber soundproofing board (A) provides excellent noise attenuation. MLV (mass-loaded vinyl) sheeting (B) can double a wall's soundproofing value. Type G drywall screws (C) have coarse threads to hold drywall panels together as the panel adhesive (D) sets to create a strong bond. Acoustical caulk (E) seals gaps to absorb noise vibrations. And for added protection, install closed cell foam gaskets (F) behind electrical coverplates.

Tools & Materials ▶

Tape measure	Type G
Screwgun or ⅜" drill	drywall screws
Caulk gun	Acoustical caulk
Drywall panels	Panel Adhesive

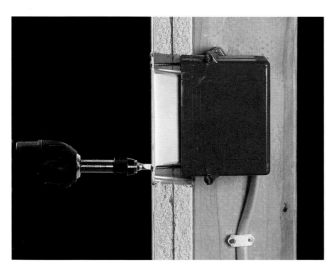

Building Code requires that the front face of electrical boxes be flush with the finished wall surface. In new construction, attach boxes so they extend past the framing of the combined thickness of the drywall layers. If you're covering an old surface, use extension rings to bring existing boxes flush.

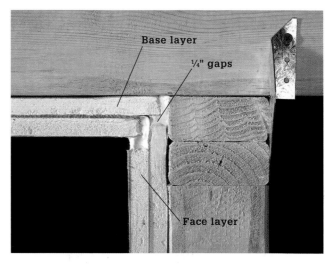

At inside corners, including wall-to-ceiling joints, stagger the joints between the layers, leaving a ¼" gap between panels. Seal all gaps with acoustical caulk to help absorb sound vibration.

How to Hang Multiple Layers of Drywall

Install the base layer of drywall or soundproofing board parallel to the framing, using the screws and spacing found on page 47. Leave a ¼" gap around the perimeter of each surface (at corners, ceilings, and along floors). After panels are installed, seal the perimeter gaps with acoustical caulk.

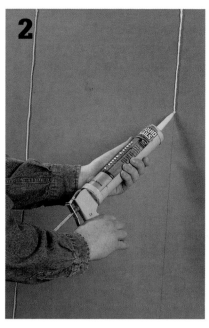

To install the face layer, use adhesive to ensure a strong bond to the base. Apply ⅜" beads of adhesive every 16" across the backside of the panels.

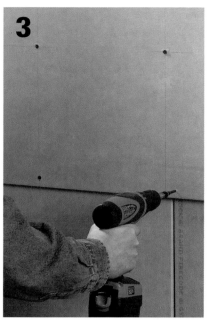

Install the face layer of drywall perpendicular to the framing and joints of the base layer, spacing screws as recommended on page 47. Make sure to stagger the seams between layers. Use Type G screws to temporarily hold panels together as the adhesive sets up.

Seal the perimeter gaps at corners, ceiling and along floors with acoustical caulk. Also seal around electrical boxes and HVAC ducts.

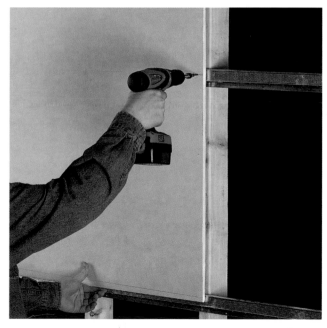

Variation: If you're installing drywall to resilient steel channels (see page 127), install the base layer panels perpendicular to the channels, and the face layer perpendicular to the base layer. For both layers, use Type S screws driven into the channels only, not into the framing.

Profiled Panels

Another option for adding decorative detail to walls and ceilings is to use designer drywall. When installed, these panels replicate the look of raised panel walls and ceilings. Designer drywall can be used to add a wainscot, bring interest to upper walls, or create a coffered ceiling.

Designer drywall is installed like standard drywall, though the layout must be carefully planned. The raised panels need to be in alignment across the entire surface to look right. Standard drywall is used to fill strips between or around panels, and all seams are finished using standard techniques. Do not get compound in the raised-panel area of drywall. If you do, carefully clean it out immediately with a clean drywall knife and a damp towel.

Tools & Materials ▸

Tape measure	Drywall screws
T-square	Taping knives
Utility knife	Mason's line
Caulk gun	Nails
Screwgun or ⅜" drill	Hammer
Designer	Finishing materials
drywall panels	Standard
Construction	drywall panels
adhesive	Corner bead

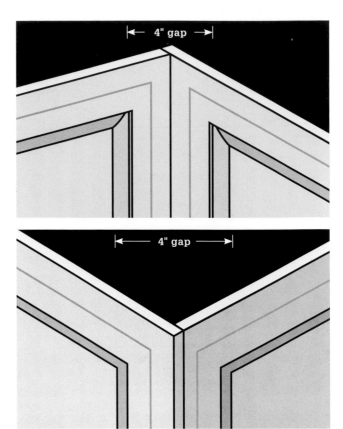

Treat both inside and outside corners similarly, so that the raised areas fall the same distance from the corner on each side of the wall. Panels also can be installed to "wrap" inside corners if necessary (see variation on page 133). Take careful measurements of your walls and ceilings and make accurate sketches to guide your project.

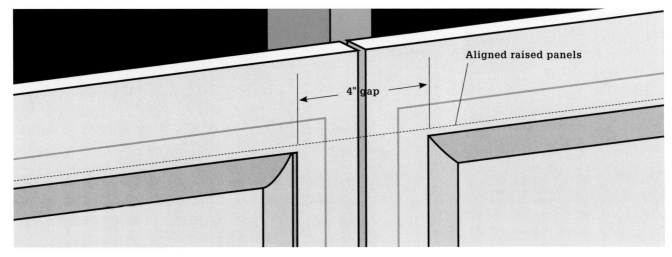

When planning your designer drywall installation, the key to a good layout is symmetry. Panels should be installed so the raised areas break at equal distances from the corners. Standard drywall can be used to fill in between panels to create a workable layout.

How to Install Decorative Drywall Panels

Measure and mark the location of the first panel on the framing. At one end of the wall, measure and mark the top edge of the panel's raised area. Drive a nail and run a level mason's line across the wall 1" from the framing. Install the first panel with drywall screws, so the top edge of the raised area is level with the mason's line.

Install subsequent panels so the raised top edge is level with the mason's line. Also leave an equal distance between the sides of the raised areas of each panel. At corners, make sure to account for panel overlap when making cuts.

Variation: To wrap an inside corner, score the back of a panel using a T-square and sharp utility knife, being careful not to pierce the front face of the panel. Gently snap back the panel, leaving the face paper intact. Fill the void with a bead of adhesive to reinforce the panel, then install it immediately.

After all designer panels are installed, finish the rest of the wall and fill gaps with standard drywall of the same thickness. The designer panels can be taped and finished in the same manner as standard drywall. At outside corners, install corner bead.

Archways

While an arch may be framed and drywalled on site, polyurethane inserts create a symmetrical arch in the style of your choosing much more easily, making them popular among pros and DIYers alike. This arch was ordered to fit, so no further cutting or fitting was needed. Note that polyurethane products carve and sand like wood, so it's better to run thicker rather than thinner when attempting to match your wall thickness.

A framed and drywalled archway divides a large space into smaller, more intimate space and makes a dramatic design statement in the process.

Tools & Materials ▸

Work gloves
Eye protection
Framing lumber
Hammer and nails
Drywall panels
Screwgun

Drywall screws
Arch inserts
Panel adhesive
Corner bead
Finishing materials

Where to cut in? ▸

If you are simply adding an arch to an existing passageway, use a hacksaw and utility knife to cut free corner bead in the area that will receive the arch inserts. Prying out bead will leave an indent for tape and mud. Leave enough corner bead at the sides so arch overlaps bead by about ¾".

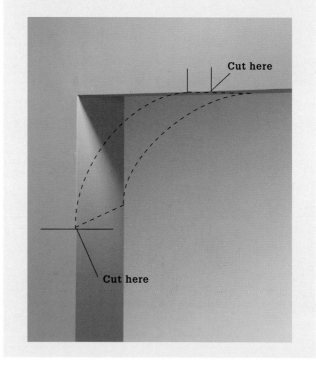

How to Build an Archway

Frame a partition wall with the alcove opening roughed in as a rectangle. Secure the frame so it is plumb and square to the ceiling joists, the adjacent wall studs (if possible), and to the floor.

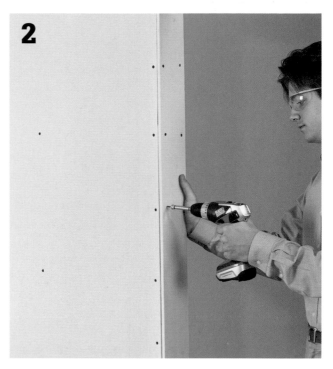

Attach drywall to all surfaces of the framed partition wall except the bottom of the door header. Avoid creating a drywall seam on the king stud.

Install corner beads and arches so the arch inserts will overlap the bead by ¾". Typically, arches are secured with panel adhesive and screws.

Tape, fill, and finish all seams, exposed fastener heads, and corners of the partition wall. Trim and finish the arched partition wall to match existing walls.

Preformed Domes

Domes and other three-dimensional features may be ordered preformed. The one we installed here is made of polyurethane. The most difficult and critical steps in dome installation involve the modifications you must make to the ceiling framing. Joists under a roof and the bottom chords of roof trusses are often under tension since the split-leg action of roof rafters pushes out against the walls on which they rest. Joists lower in the building may be supporting tremendous loads that aren't obvious. Therefore, before you cut through structural members, you must have a framing-modification plan drawn up by a qualified structural engineer. In most localities, these drawings need to be approved by a building inspector in order to get a building permit to do the work.

Tools & Materials ▸

Work gloves
Eye protection
Compass
Straightedge
Screwgun
Drywall screws
Framing lumber
Spiral saw
Insulation (if necessary)

Light fixture
Caulk
Finishing materials

A simple domed shape transforms an ordinary ceiling into a grand design statement, especially when the dome is appointed with an attractive ceiling light or chandelier. This Fypon dome (see Resources, page 156) is fabricated from urethane foam and installed as one piece.

Preformed Dome Styles

A plain round dome is hard to beat for versatility and ease of installation. This fabricated dome does require that you either remove sections of ceiling joist or create a lower ceiling with a furred-out framework.

Ornate domes add high drama, especially when they include a chandelier or an intricate medallion.

How to Install a Preformed Dome

Trace the dome onto cardboard in an upside-down position and transfer four alignment lines onto the outline. Since this outline includes the flange, it's larger than the hole you need to cut in the ceiling.

Scribe a second, smaller circle inside the outline by setting a compass or scribe slightly less than the width of the flange and following along the outline. Use a straightedge and marker to connect the opposite alignment marks, forming a cross. Cut out the inside circle to make your template.

Screw the cardboard template to the ceiling. The alignment cross may be used to center a round dome or to make an oval dome parallel with a wall. Transfer the alignment marks to the ceiling with a pencil to guide positioning of the domes that are oval or imperfectly round.

Cut through the drywall and framing at the edge of the template. Add re-enforcement framing as specified by a qualified structural engineer. Add trimmers and blocking to the dome edges at screw locations. Add insulation if necessary, above the dome.

Prepare for a fixture box if a light fixture or fan will be hung in the dome. Drill a 1" hole in the center of the dome. Raise framing above the ceiling opening to secure an electric fixture box above the center of the opening. Dome specifications will determine how far to recess the fixture box from the face of the ceiling. Typically, the face of the fixture box should be flush with the finished (visible) face of the dome. You may temporarily attach the dome to help position the fixture box.

Cut a hole for the light fixture wiring in the center of the dome. A hole saw that's slightly bigger than the round electrical fixture box works. For larger or more challenging openings, use a spiral saw to cut the outline of the fixture box in the dome.

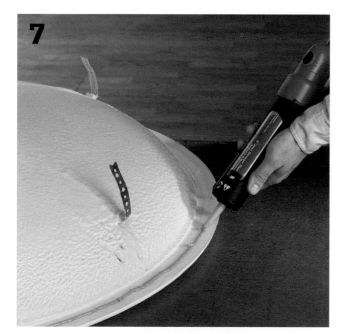

Apply polyurethane construction adhesive to the back of the dome flange. Lift the dome into place with helpers, aligning the ceiling and dome alignment marks and fitting the dome around the electrical box. Attach the flange of the dome to the blocking through the ceiling with drywall screws. Countersink the screw heads slightly.

Hang your light or fan and caulk all air gaps through and around the fixture box. Caulk the seam where the dome flange meets the ceiling. Cover the fastener heads with joint compound. Finish the dome with ceiling paint.

Repairs

Fixing physical damage to drywall is fairly straightforward, and you'll find many drywall repair products available for sale in hardware stores and online. But most damage can be patched with just a small piece of drywall, some finishing supplies, and a bit of spackle and paint. The tricky part of the job is getting the repair to blend in with the surrounding wall or ceiling. Unless you have some leftover paint from the surrounding surface and the paint job is less than a year old, your finished repair may not blend in as seamlessly as you'd like. You can try to have new paint color-matched at the paint store if you bring in a sample of the wall color (not always easy to obtain). You can also feather in the paint around the edges, so the transition is less obvious. However, in some cases you may need to repaint the entire wall to the corners to hide the difference. Be careful here, as you'll quickly face a slippery slope: do you repaint the adjoining wall to blend with the wall you painted to blend with the repair? The chain can go on for some time.

In this chapter:

- Drywall Repairs
- Plaster Repairs
- Ceiling Repairs
- Water-Damaged Walls & Ceilings Repairs

Drywall Repairs

Patching holes and concealing popped nails are common drywall repairs. Small holes can be filled directly, but larger patches must be supported with some kind of backing, such as plywood. To repair holes left by nails or screws, dimple the hole slightly with the handle of a utility knife or taping knife and fill it with spackle or joint compound.

Use joint tape anywhere the drywall's face paper or joint tape has torn or peeled away. Always cut away any loose drywall material, face paper or joint tape from the damaged area, trimming back to solid drywall material.

All drywall repairs require three coats of joint compound, just as in new installations. Lightly sand your repairs before painting or adding texture.

Tools & Materials ▸

Drill or screwgun	150-grit sandpaper
Hammer	Wood scraps
Utility knife	Paper joint tape
Taping knives	Self-adhesive
Framing square	fiberglass mesh
Drywall saw	joint tape
Hacksaw	Drywall repair patch
Fine metal file	Drywall repair clips
1¼" drywall screws	Corner bead
Lightweight spackle	Paintable latex
All-purpose	or silicone culk
joint compound	Drywall wet sander

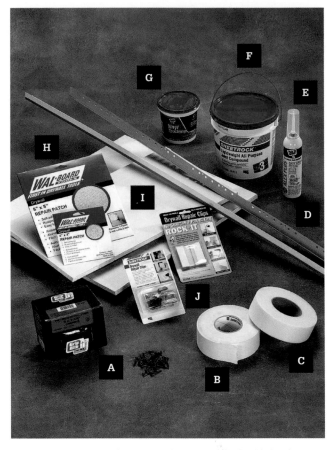

Most drywall problems can be remedied with basic dry wall materials and specialty materials: drywall screws (A); paper joint tape (B); self-adhesive fiberglass mesh tape (C); corner bead (D); paintable latex or silicone caulk (E); all-purpose joint compound (F); lightweight spackling compound (G); drywall repair patches (H); scraps of drywall (I); and drywall repair clips (J).

To repair a popped nail, drive a drywall screw 2" above or below the nail, so it pulls the panel tight to the framing. Scrape away loose paint or compound, then drive the popped nail ¹⁄₁₆" below the surface. Apply three coats of joint compound to cover the holes.

If drywall is dented, without cracks or tears in the face paper, just fill the hole with lightweight spackling or all-purpose joint compound, let it dry, and sand it smooth.

How to Repair Cracks & Gashes

1

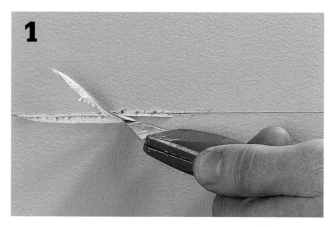

Use a utility knife to cut away loose drywall or face paper and widen the crack into a "V"; the notch will help hold the joint compound.

2

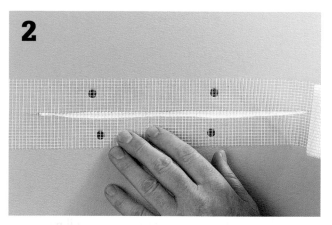

Push along the sides of the crack with your hand. If the drywall moves, secure the panel with 1¼" drywall screws driven into the nearest framing members. Cover the crack and screws with self-adhesive mesh tape.

3

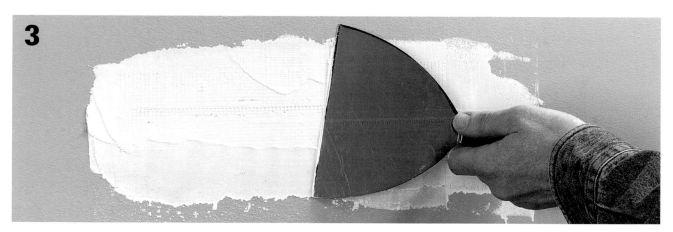

Cover the tape with compound, lightly forcing it into the mesh, then smooth it off, leaving just enough to conceal the tape. Add two more coats, in successively broader and thinner coats to blend the patch into the surrounding area.

4

For cracks at corners or ceilings, cut through the existing seam and cut away any loose drywall material or tape, then apply a new length of tape or inside-corner bead and two coats of joint compound.

Variation: For small cracks at corners, apply a thin bead of paintable latex or silicone caulk over the crack, then use your finger to smooth the caulk into the corner.

How to Patch Small Holes in Drywall

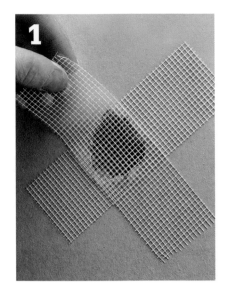

1

Trim away any broken drywall, face paper, or joint tape around the hole using a utility knife. Cover the hole with crossed strips of self-adhesive mesh tape.

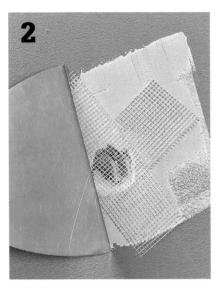

2

Cover the tape with all-purpose joint compound, lightly forcing it into the mesh, then smooth it off, leaving just enough to conceal the tape.

3

Add two more coats of compound in successively broader and thinner coats to blend the patch into the surrounding area. Use a drywall wet sander to smooth the repair area.

Other Options for Patching Small Holes in Drywall

Drywall repair patches: Cover the damaged area with the self-adhesive patch; the thin metal plate provides support and the fiberglass mesh helps hold the joint compound.

Beveled drywall patch: Bevel the edges of the hole with a drywall saw, then cut a drywall patch to fit. Trim the beveled patch until it fits tight and flush with the panel surface. Apply plenty of compound to the beveled edges, then push the patch into the hole. Finish with paper tape and three coats of compound.

Drywall paper-flange patch: Cut a drywall patch a couple inches larger than the hole. Mark the hole on the backside of the patch, then score and snap along the lines. Remove the waste material, keeping the face paper "flange" intact. Apply compound around the hole, insert the patch, and embed the flange into the compound. Finish with two additional coats.

How to Patch Large Holes in Drywall

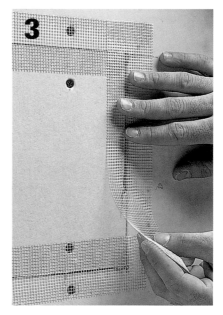

Outline the damaged area using a framing square. (Cutting four right angles makes it easier to measure and cut the patch.) Use a drywall saw to cut along the outline.

Cut plywood or lumber backer strips a few inches longer than the height of the cutout. Fasten the strips to the back side of the drywall using 1¼" drywall screws.

Cut a drywall patch ⅛" smaller than the cutout dimensions and fasten it to the backer strips with screws. Apply mesh joint tape over the seams. Finish the seams with three coats of compound.

How to Patch Large Holes with Repair Clips

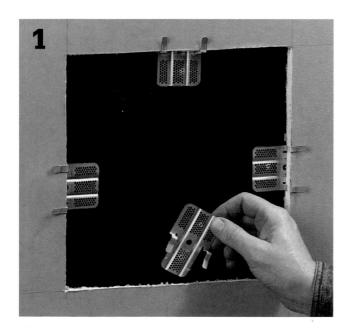

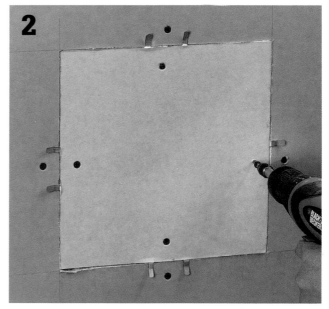

Cut out the damaged area using a drywall saw. Center one repair clip on each edge of the hole. Using the provided drywall screws, drive one screw through the wall and into the clips; position the screws ¾" from the edge and centered between the clip's tabs.

Cut a new drywall patch to fit in the hole. Fasten the patch to the clips, placing drywall screws adjacent to the previous screw locations and ¾" from the edge. Remove the tabs from the clips, then finish the joints with tape and three coats of compound.

Ceiling Repairs

Holes and cracks in ceilings can be repaired the same way walls are, but other ceiling problems require different solutions. Sagging panels must be refastened or replaced. Damaged acoustical tiles need to be removed and new tiles pieced in. And textures such as acoustical "popcorn" that flake off have to be scraped and resprayed, or simply removed altogether.

Plaster ceilings can be more difficult to work with. While minor repairs are manageable, widespread failure of the bond between the plaster coating and the lath foundation can be dangerous. If you find large spongy areas or extensive sags in your plaster ceiling, replace the area (see pages 92 to 97) or consult a professional.

Aerosol touch-up products are available for small repairs to ceilings with popcorn and orange peel textures. Use a taping knife to scrap away the existing texture at the damaged area and slightly around it. Make any necessary repairs, then spray on the aerosol texture carefully to blend the new texture with the existing ceiling.

How to Remove Popcorn Ceiling Texture

1

To protect floors and ease cleanup later, line floors with 6-mil plastic, then cover with corrugated cardboard to provide a non-slip surface. Caution: popcorn ceilings in houses built prior to 1980 may contain asbestos. Contact your local building department for regulations governing asbestos removal.

2

Using a pressure sprayer, dampen the ceiling with a mixture of a teaspoon of liquid detergent per gallon of water. Allow 20 minutes for the mixture to soak in, rewetting as necessary.

3

Scrape texture from the ceiling using a 6" taping knife. Be careful not to cut into the drywall surface. After all texture is removed, sand rough spots, then carefully roll up and dispose of the plastic and debris. Patch any damaged areas with joint compound, then prime and paint.

How to Replace Acoustical Ceiling Tile

Cut out the center section of the damaged tile with a utility knife. Slide the edges away from the surrounding tiles.

Trim the upper lip of the grooved edges of the new tile with a utility knife and straightedge. If necessary, also remove one of the tongues.

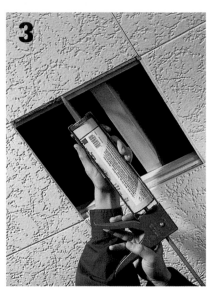

At the ceiling, apply construction adhesive to the furring strips. Install the new tile, tongue first, and press it into the adhesive. *Tip: To hold large tiles in place while the glue dries, lay a flat board across the tile, then prop a 2 × 4 post between the board and the floor.*

How to Raise a Sagging Drywall Ceiling

Position a T-brace under the lowest point of the sagging area with the bottom end on a piece of plywood or hardboard on the floor. Nudge it forward until the sagging panels are tight to the joists. If fasteners pop through the surface, drive them back in.

Remove loose tape and compound at joints between loose panels. Starting at one end, drive drywall screws with fender washers every 4" through the center of the joint and into the joists. In the field of the panel, drive screws 2" from existing fasteners.

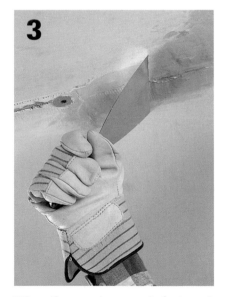

When the area is securely fastened, remove the T-brace. Scrape off any loose chips of paint or drywall around joints and screws, then fill with compound. Cover large cracks or gaps with drywall tape before applying the compound.

Water-Damaged Walls & Ceilings Repairs

A sure sign of a water problem is discoloration and bubbling on the ceiling surface. Water from a leaky roof or pipe above will quickly find a low spot or a joint between drywall panels, soaking through to a visible surface in a matter of minutes. Water in joints is especially damaging because it ruins the edges of two panels at once. If you have a water problem, be sure to fix the leak and allow the damaged drywall to dry thoroughly before making any repairs.

Whenever water or moisture infiltrates a house, there is always a concern regarding mold. Mold grows where water and nutrients are present—damp drywall paper can provide such an environment. You can use a damp rag and baking soda or a small amount of diluted household bleach to clean up small areas of mold (less than one square yard), though you should wear goggles, rubber gloves, and a dust mask to prevent contact with mold spores. If mold occupies more area than this, you may have a more serious problem. Contact a mold abatement specialist for assessment and remediation. To help prevent mold growth, use exhaust fans and dehumidifiers to rid your home of excess moisture and repair plumbing leaks as soon as they are found.

If damaged drywall requires extensive repair, resurfacing walls and ceilings with a layer of new drywall may be the best option. Resurfacing is essentially the same as hanging multiple layers of drywall, and results in a smooth, flat surface. However, the added wall thickness can affect the appearance of window and door trim, which may need to be extended. Use ⅜" drywall for resurfacing—though ¼" drywall is thinner, it is fragile and can be difficult to work with.

Tools & Materials ▸

Work gloves	Joint compound
Eye protection	Drywall
Drywall saw	(for patching
Utility knife	or resurfacing)
Drill or screwgun	Panel adhesive
Taping knives	Stain-blocking
Paint roller and tray	primer/sealer
Drywall screws	Paper tape

How to Repair Water-Damaged Drywall

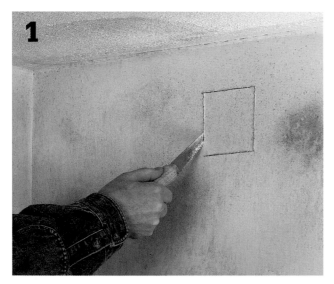

1

After the source for the water leak has been fixed, cut 4" holes at each end of joist and stud bays to help ventilation. Remove wet or damp insulation to prevent continuing mold growth. Use fans and dehumidifiers to help speed up the drying process.

2

Remove loose tape and compound using a utility knife. Cut back areas of soft drywall to solid material. To prevent sagging, prop water-damaged ceiling panels against joists with T-braces (see page 151).

3

Once drywall is dry, refasten ceiling panels to framing or remove panels that are excessively bowed. Reinforce damaged wall panels with drywall screws driven 2" from the existing fasteners.

Mold Remedy ▶

If drywall contains small areas (less than one square yard) of mold on the panel surface, clean with a damp rag and baking soda or diluted household bleach. Allow to dry, then continue the repair. Wear protective eyewear, rubber gloves, and a disposable dust mask when cleaning mold. Caution: larger areas containing mold should be evaluated and treated by a mold abatement specialist.

4

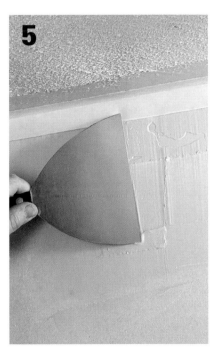

Patch all vent holes and damaged areas with drywall (see pages 142 to 146). Apply a quality stain-blocking primer/sealer to the affected area. Use an oil- or shellac-based sealer; latex-based sealers may allow water stains to bleed through.

5

After the primer/sealer has dried, finish all joints and repairs with paper tape and three coats of compound. If water stains bleed through, reseal prior to final priming and painting.

Variation: Where damage is severe, replace the panels or resurface with a new layer of ⅜" drywall. Hang new panels perpendicular to existing drywall using panel adhesive to strengthen the bond. See pages 128 to 129 for more information on hanging multiple layers of drywall.

Conversions

Metric Conversions

To Convert:	To:	Multiply by:
Inches	Millimeters	25.4
Inches	Centimeters	2.54
Feet	Meters	0.305
Yards	Meters	0.914
Square inches	Square centimeters	6.45
Square feet	Square meters	0.093
Square yards	Square meters	0.836
Ounces	Milliliters	30.0
Pints (U.S.)	Liters	0.473 (Imp. 0.568)
Quarts (U.S.)	Liters	0.946 (Imp. 1.136)
Gallons (U.S.)	Liters	3.785 (Imp. 4.546)
Ounces	Grams	28.4
Pounds	Kilograms	0.454

To Convert:	To:	Multiply by:
Millimeters	Inches	0.039
Centimeters	Inches	0.394
Meters	Feet	3.28
Meters	Yards	1.09
Square centimeters	Square inches	0.155
Square meters	Square feet	10.8
Square meters	Square yards	1.2
Milliliters	Ounces	.033
Liters	Pints (U.S.)	2.114 (Imp. 1.76)
Liters	Quarts (U.S.)	1.057 (Imp. 0.88)
Liters	Gallons (U.S.)	0.264 (Imp. 0.22)
Grams	Ounces	0.035
Kilograms	Pounds	2.2

Converting Temperatures

Convert degrees Fahrenheit (F) to degrees Celsius (C) by following this simple formula: Subtract 32 from the Fahrenheit temperature reading. Then, multiply that number by $5/9$. For example, 77°F - 32 = 45. 45 × $5/9$ = 25°C.

To convert degrees Celsius to degrees Fahrenheit, multiply the Celsius temperature reading by $9/5$. Then, add 32. For example, 25°C × $9/5$ = 45. 45 + 32 = 77°F.

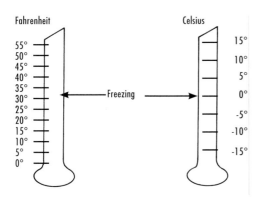

Metric Plywood Panels

Metric plywood panels are commonly available in two sizes: 1,200 mm × 2,400 mm and 1,220 mm × 2,400 mm, which is roughly equivalent to a 4 × 8-ft. sheet. Standard and Select sheathing panels come in standard thicknesses, while Sanded grade panels are available in special thicknesses.

Standard Sheathing Grade		Sanded Grade	
7.5 mm	($5/16$ in.)	6 mm	($4/17$ in.)
9.5 mm	($3/8$ in.)	8 mm	($5/16$ in.)
12.5 mm	($1/2$ in.)	11 mm	($7/16$ in.)
15.5 mm	($5/8$ in.)	14 mm	($9/16$ in.)
18.5 mm	($3/4$ in.)	17 mm	($2/3$ in.)
20.5 mm	($13/16$ in.)	19 mm	($3/4$ in.)
22.5 mm	($7/8$ in.)	21 mm	($13/16$ in.)
25.5 mm	(1 in.)	24 mm	($15/16$ in.)

Lumber Dimensions

Nominal - U.S.	Actual - U.S. (in inches)	Metric
1 × 2	$3/4$ × $1\frac{1}{2}$	19 × 38 mm
1 × 3	$3/4$ × $2\frac{1}{2}$	19 × 64 mm
1 × 4	$3/4$ × $3\frac{1}{2}$	19 × 89 mm
1 × 5	$3/4$ × $4\frac{1}{2}$	19 × 114 mm
1 × 6	$3/4$ × $5\frac{1}{2}$	19 × 140 mm
1 × 7	$3/4$ × $6\frac{1}{4}$	19 × 159 mm
1 × 8	$3/4$ × $7\frac{1}{4}$	19 × 184 mm
1 × 10	$3/4$ × $9\frac{1}{4}$	19 × 235 mm
1 × 12	$3/4$ × $11\frac{1}{4}$	19 × 286 mm
$1\frac{1}{4}$ × 4	1 × $3\frac{1}{2}$	25 × 89 mm
$1\frac{1}{4}$ × 6	1 × $5\frac{1}{2}$	25 × 140 mm
$1\frac{1}{4}$ × 8	1 × $7\frac{1}{4}$	25 × 184 mm
$1\frac{1}{4}$ × 10	1 × $9\frac{1}{4}$	25 × 235 mm
$1\frac{1}{4}$ × 12	1 × $11\frac{1}{4}$	25 × 286 mm
$1\frac{1}{2}$ × 4	$1\frac{1}{4}$ × $3\frac{1}{2}$	32 × 89 mm
$1\frac{1}{2}$ × 6	$1\frac{1}{4}$ × $5\frac{1}{2}$	32 × 140 mm
$1\frac{1}{2}$ × 8	$1\frac{1}{4}$ × $7\frac{1}{4}$	32 × 184 mm
$1\frac{1}{2}$ × 10	$1\frac{1}{4}$ × $9\frac{1}{4}$	32 × 235 mm
$1\frac{1}{2}$ × 12	$1\frac{1}{4}$ × $11\frac{1}{4}$	32 × 286 mm
2 × 4	$1\frac{1}{2}$ × $3\frac{1}{2}$	38 × 89 mm
2 × 6	$1\frac{1}{2}$ × $5\frac{1}{2}$	38 × 140 mm
2 × 8	$1\frac{1}{2}$ × $7\frac{1}{4}$	38 × 184 mm
2 × 10	$1\frac{1}{2}$ × $9\frac{1}{4}$	38 × 235 mm
2 × 12	$1\frac{1}{2}$ × $11\frac{1}{4}$	38 × 286 mm
3 × 6	$2\frac{1}{2}$ × $5\frac{1}{2}$	64 × 140 mm
4 × 4	$3\frac{1}{2}$ × $3\frac{1}{2}$	89 × 89 mm
4 × 6	$3\frac{1}{2}$ × $5\frac{1}{2}$	89 × 140 mm

Liquid Measurement Equivalents

1 Pint	= 16 Fluid Ounces	= 2 Cups
1 Quart	= 32 Fluid Ounces	= 2 Pints
1 Gallon	= 128 Fluid Ounces	= 4 Quarts

Drill Bit Guide

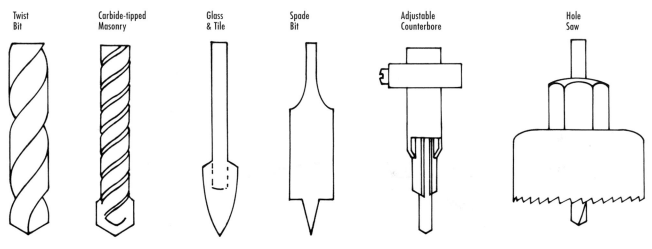

Twist Bit

Carbide-tipped Masonry

Glass & Tile

Spade Bit

Adjustable Counterbore

Hole Saw

Nails

Nail lengths are identified by numbers from 4 to 60 followed by the letter "d," which stands for "penny." For general framing and repair work, use common or box nails. Common nails are best suited to framing work where strength is important. Box nails are smaller in diameter than common nails, which makes them easier to drive and less likely to split wood. Use box nails for light work and thin materials. Most common and box nails have a cement or vinyl coating that improves their holding power.

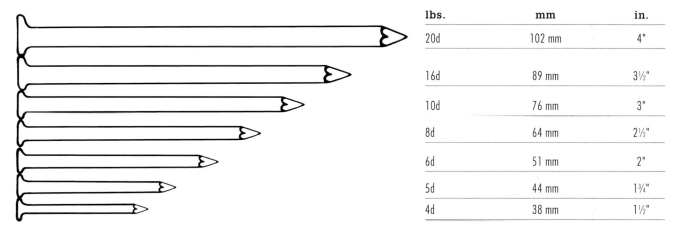

lbs.	mm	in.
20d	102 mm	4"
16d	89 mm	3½"
10d	76 mm	3"
8d	64 mm	2½"
6d	51 mm	2"
5d	44 mm	1¾"
4d	38 mm	1½"

Counterbore, Shank & Pilot Hole Diameters

Screw Size	Counterbore Diameter for Screw Head (in inches)	Clearance Hole for Screw Shank (in inches)	Pilot Hole Diameter	
			Hard Wood (in inches)	Soft Wood (in inches)
#1	9/64	5/64	3/64	1/32
#2	1/4	3/32	3/64	1/32
#3	1/4	7/64	1/16	3/64
#4	1/4	1/8	1/16	3/64
#5	1/4	1/8	5/64	1/16
#6	5/16	9/64	3/32	5/64
#7	5/16	5/32	3/32	5/64
#8	3/8	11/64	1/8	3/32
#9	3/8	11/64	1/8	3/32
#10	3/8	3/16	1/8	7/64
#11	1/2	3/16	5/32	9/64
#12	1/2	7/32	9/64	1/8

Resources

3M
Masking Paper and 3M Hand-Masker, page 86
888-364-3577
www.3m.com

Black & Decker Corp.
Power tools
800-544-6986
www.blackanddecker.com

Fypon Ltd.
Urethane Millwork, page 136
800-446-3040
www.fypon.com

The Steel Network, Inc.
Curved Steel Track, page 110
888-474-4876
www.steelnetwork.com

Photography Credits

p. 6–7 (all) iStock Photo
p. 8–9 Fypon / www.fypon.com / 800 446 9373
p. 10 Photolibrary / www.photolibrary.com
p. 11–12 Fypon
p. 13 (top) Fypon, (lower) Photolibrary
p. 16 iStock Photo

p. 61 iStock Photo
p. 92–93 (top) USG Corp. / www.usg.com / 800 950 3839
p. 109 iStock Photo
p. 110 (lower) iStock Photo
p. 114 (left) © Karen Melvin Photography
p. 137 Fypon

Index

CREATIVE PUBLISHING international

NOTE TO READERS

The DVD disk included with this book is offered as a free premium to buyers of this book.

The live video demonstrations are designed to be viewed on electronic devices suitable for viewing standard DVD video discs, including most television DVD players, as well as a Mac or PC computer equipped with a DVD-compatible disc drive and standard multi-media software.

In addition, your DVD-compatible computer will allow you to read the electronic version of the book. The electronic version is provided in a standard PDF form, which is readable by any software compatible with that format, including Adobe Reader.

To access the electronic pages, open the directory of your computer's DVD drive, and click on the icon with the image of this book cover.

The electronic book carries the same copyright restrictions as the print version. You are welcome to use it in any way that is useful for you, including printing the pages for your own use. You can also loan the disc to friends or family members, much the way you would loan a printed book.

However, we do request that you respect copyright law and the integrity of this book by not attempting to make electronic copies of this disc, or by distributing the files electronically via the internet.

Creative Publishing international

400 First Avenue North • Suite 300 • Minneapolis, MN 55401 • 800-328-0590, opt 2 • www.creativepub.com